Bondhu

SEAGULL
BOOKS
•
CELEBRATING
40 YEARS

THE INDIA LIST

Bondhu

My Father, My Friend

KUNAL SEN

LONDON NEW YORK CALCUTTA

Seagull Books, 2023

Text © Kunal Sen, 2023
Photos © Individual photographers and/or their estates

First published by Seagull Books, 2023

ISBN 978 1 80309 317 8

British Library Cataloguing-in-Publication Data
A catalogue record for this book is available from the British Library.

Typeset by Seagull Books, Calcutta, India
Printed and bound by Hyam Enterprises, Calcutta, India

To Ma, Bondhu and Anu
Who unintentionally taught me how to read life
and tell stories

CONTENTS

Acknowledgements

I grew up among three great storytellers, each with their own style, each jostling for attention, each compelling in their own way. I was left with two options: turn into a quiet listener, or quickly develop my own storytelling skills. I guess I chose the latter. I may never achieve the same level of intensity, but was perhaps good enough to be heard in that bazaar of brilliant hawkers.

I had not seriously thought of telling my family's story until one afternoon, a year after my father's death, sitting in the fascinating office of Seagull Books, our family friend Naveen Kishore mentioned the possibility. Apart from writing a few scattered memories, I had not considered putting it all together. The idea gained strength as I slowly realized that many of my memories would disappear unless I put them on paper. Finally, in 2022, I carved out some time from my busy life comprising a demanding job, my art practice and my passion for books. After ten months of sporadic writing, I finally had a manuscript.

I knew from the very start that most people who would read this book would already be somewhat familiar with my father's life. Therefore, I decided not to follow chronological story but to break up the narrative into thematic chapters.

During this process, my wife, Nisha, read each chapter as it was written, and like any spouse with fifty years of acquaintance, was brutally honest and insightful. I could not have finished this project without her constant feedback.

Even though the main readership of the book will comprise people familiar with my father's work, I also wanted feedback from people who have little or no contact with his films or the culture I grew up in. In this regard, I am thankful to Yangzi Xu and Lise McKean for their time and valuable remarks. The first person to read the book in its entirety was my friend, Prof. Dipesh Chakraborty; his encouraging remarks and advice proved very helpful.

I am particularly grateful to Megan Michel for her going over the manuscript with a keen and professional eye. Finally, the book would not have happened without the professional care and attention of Sunandini Banerjee and her team at Seagull Books.

The photographs I have included are mostly from our family albums. Cameras were not ubiquitous when I grew up, so there are very few images, especially from my childhood. Most of the photographs were taken by either my father, my wife Nisha, her sister Jagriti, Subhash Nandy, Nemai Ghosh, and a few others whose identity is lost in time.

Ever since I have finished the manuscript, whenever I think about it, I realize I have missed so many more anecdotes and people. A few hundred pages cannot fully capture a lifetime of interaction. To anyone not represented here, and who should be, I apologize.

PART 1

Bondhu

FIRST BONDING

My earliest memories do not prominently feature my father. They are mostly of my mother and my uncle, Anu. My father's world was always a little distant, a world where he was engrossed with his friends, his ideas and perhaps himself. That is not to say he did not love me, but that there were other priorities. He realized that I was cared for without his active participation, which relieved him.

My mother told me that when I was just a few months old, a minor earthquake occurred in Calcutta. We lived on the southern part of the city, on Ashwini Dutta Road, in a one-room flat on the top floor of a three-storey building. As the floor shook, everyone panicked. After all, earthquakes were infrequent in that part of the world. I was lying on the floor on a layer of folded clothes which served as my infant bed. My father responded to the quake by swiftly kneeling over my tiny body, on all fours, in an attempt to protect me from falling debris, ready to take the hit on his bare back. Despite the confusion and chaos, it didn't escape my mother that his self-sacrificial act was in fact not so safe for me! The last thing she wanted was to have her infant son smothered by the full weight of an adult body. She gave a shout, and my father, relieved that he had adequately demonstrated his responsibility as a father, moved away at the same time as the tremors subsided.

However, there were moments when we did bond as father and son. My earliest memory is of a wintry morning when I was probably four years old. Winters in Calcutta are brief, lasting only a few weeks and mild by any global standard. Still, they have a distinct charm, and are a welcome relief from the tyranny of tropical heat and humidity. That morning, even before the sun rose, my father woke me up and asked me to get dressed. I wasn't sure what was happening, but something told me that an adventure was afoot.

I came out of our ground-floor flat on Manoharpukur Road, holding my father's hand. The sky was still inky black, the streets lit only by the dim street lamps. All the windows of the buildings were still dark, the street tranquil. We walked along for a while, though I had no idea where we were going. A few minutes later we arrived at Deshapriya Park. A gate, as high as my father's waist, had been installed to keep out stray dogs and cows. We pushed the gate forward, squeezed into the curved intermediate space, then pushed the gate back and walked in. The clank of the metal rang out loud in the early morning silence. The park was even darker than the streets. Finally, we came out at the other end and stood at the edge of a major thoroughfare—Rashbehari Avenue.

It was a two-way road, divided by a raised tramline. My father held my hand a little more firmly; we crossed over to the raised tramway and stopped at the paved part of the track. There was very little traffic and no tramcar in sight. By then, I had realized that wherever we were going, it involved a tram ride, and that idea was already sending ripples of excitement through my little body.

There was a chill in the air, and my father drew me closer to keep me warm. After what felt like a long wait, there was the faint glow of a single headlamp. The glow grew brighter. After a few more minutes, I could even hear the soft sound of the tram's bell. It slowly approached our stop and, spotting us, slowed down to a halt. We got in; the conductor pulled the cord to ring a bell in the driver's compartment to tell him it was OK to carry on. The compartment was mostly empty. As my father was about to take a seat, I softly tugged at his hand and pulled him towards the very first seat, right next to the driver's cabin. This was the only seat where one could not only see out of the left window but also straight ahead. The cold winter air was blowing in through the front window, and perhaps that is why the seat was not occupied. My father purchased the ticket from the conductor, and asked him if this was the first tram of the day. He confirmed that it was, and had set off from the terminal at four in the morning.

As the tram moved forward on its uneven rails, occasionally ringing its little bell, I stared at the lines ahead, converging at a distant point. I felt I owned the city and everything in it. The sky was growing brighter, and I could finally see the silhouettes of the buildings. After a few more minutes, the buildings grew fewer and fewer; we were moving away from the more congested parts of the city. Soon, we seemed to be in a region of dense fog, and all I could see was the faint glow of our car's internal lights reflecting on the thick haze. Right then, my father stood up and asked me to follow. I held his hand tightly and carefully walked up to the open doorway and then my father pulled the bell cord to indicate that we wanted to get off.

The tram slowed to a stop, and we both stepped out and into an utterly opaque fog. The tram rang its bell again, and resumed its journey and slowly, its taillight faded away. A few moments later, we could no longer hear the sound of its metal wheels. We could hear nothing, see nothing; there was just the fog and the shape of my father as he walked into the unknown, holding my hand. There was grass under my feet, wet with morning dew. I could make out some tree trunks here and there. After walking a few more steps, suddenly my father let go of my hand.

I turned around to take in my surroundings, and when my gaze returned to where my father had been, he was gone. The air suddenly felt colder. I could not see him, but I could still feel his presence. After a few seconds, he called out my name and suggested we play hide-and-seek. That was the best game I had played thus far in my brief life. I would tentatively run a few steps, and find myself all alone, yet know that he was there somewhere. When I began to feel lost, he would appear out of nowhere and wrap his arms around me. Moments later, I would be alone again. Unlike other games I'd played with adults, I somehow knew we were both enjoying it. It was not an adult indulging a child, but a mutual game where we both had something to gain.

The magic did not last forever. The sun came out, and the foggy landscape did not look magical any more. The place became finite and tangible, and we were no longer alone but sharing a world with other people strolling out for their morning walks on the Maidan. We took a tram back home, now more crowded and more purposeful.

That morning, in some ways, perhaps defined the relationship between my father and me. He always pushed me towards independence, towards finding my own direction while knowing that he was watching. He did not want me to get lost, but he would not be the one to show me the way.

EARLY FRIENDS

Throughout his life, my father's world revolved around his friends. Even before I was born, his absolute passion for cinema arose out of incessant addas with his friends who shared similar interests and ambitions. The circle included Ritwik Ghatak, Tapas Sen, Salil Chowdhury, Hrishikesh Mukherjee, Nripen Ganguly. At the time of their meeting and becoming friends, they were all mostly jobless, penniless dreamers, all eager to create something and possessed of an indomitable urge to change the world. They spent their days in roadside tea stalls and parks, discussing their big ideas, but had little to show. None of them had any formal training in filmmaking. But many of them carried film ideas in their kurta pockets, waiting to pounce on an unsuspecting person who might have enough money to finance a film and be willing to risk it on someone with big dreams and no experience.

It is astonishing that many of them eventually convinced someone to do exactly that. What was it that persuaded some film financers to take such a big risk? Could it be that there was a general shortage of talented people willing to step forward in those early days of post-Independence cinema? But that does not explain it all. There must have been an extraordinary passion in these people that was palpable and may have even manifested as a vague sense of confidence.

Hrishikesh Mukherjee was the first to get a meaningful apprenticeship in films, first in New Theatres Studio in Calcutta, in the camera and editing departments. Then he moved to Bombay to work with Bimal Roy before making his first independent film in the late fifties.

Ritwik Ghatak got a chance to make his first film, *Nagarik*, in the early fifties. My mother, then known as Gita Shome, played a significant role in it. My mother's involvement with Ghatak started with a small theatre group called Natya Chakra, part of the Indian People's Theatre Association (IPTA), the cultural wing of the Communist Party of India. My father, Ghatak and Bijon Bhattacharya were all part of this group, and my mother was a teenage actor in many of the plays they produced. That is when my parents got close to each other, and finally married in 1953.

My father was less successful in obtaining financing, but eventually, in 1954–55, he convinced someone to take a chance on him and made his first film, *Raat Bhore*. Whatever it was, my father never made mention of this film, and any questions about it were immediately dismissed. He was convinced that he didn't know how to make a film, and was so devastated by this attempt that he decided never to try again.

Before the launch of their film careers, none of the friends had any meaningful income. They somehow managed with support from their families, all of whom were desperately poor. My father would tell me stories about him and Ritwik Ghatak. Both of them were once walking down a street. After turning into a lane, Ritwik-kaka pulled my father back—because he'd spotted someone whom he owed some money. Just as they turned away and began to walk down another street, this time my father pulled Ritwik-kaka back—because there was another money lender on this street that *he* was trying to avoid. I'd even heard that Ritwik-kaka had a substantial debt to a bidi vendor, even though in those days each bundle of the hand-made cigarettes cost just a few paisa.

One must ask, what was the source of their conviction that gave them the strength to endure this poverty? What made them so determined not to take up a salaried job but to continue dreaming? I think part of it was their political convictions. They firmly believed that the state of society was unjust and unfair, but they also believed that it could be changed and that change was imminent. Such optimism may seem naive now, but that was an age of idealism, and all of them were smitten with that ideal. There was also the strength each of them gave and received to and from the others. I doubt they could have soldiered on if they were in it alone. Each of them was just as poor, just as motivated to change the world and just as convinced that the change would happen. Very few of their friends had chosen the more accepted career paths, and therefore the choices they made seemed somewhat normal to them.

I heard a story from my mother about how, right after she and my father got married, they moved to a room on the roof—known in Bengali as chilekothha—and did not have anything substantial to eat for a couple of days. Then one afternoon my mother insisted my father do something about their situation. He promised to borrow some money, buy some rice and come back immediately. My mother believed him, and decided to start the coal-fired stove since it took quite some time for the fire and heat to build up. As the coals began to glow red, she put her rice-cooking handi on the fire and put the water to boil. Any moment now, she thought, my father would return with some rice—but there was no sign of him. My mother began to feel sorry for him, perhaps desperately begging someone for money. So she kept adding water to the pot, letting it boil over and over as she waited for his return.

Suddenly she heard a knock on the door. Opening it, she saw it was one of his friends, Nripen. He asked if Mrinal was home. My mother explained that he had gone out a while ago to do some shopping. Nripen immediately corrected her—my father had been chatting with him and some other friends in the neighbourhood park. He had excused himself a little while ago and then not returned. So Nripen was wondering if he had come back home. When Nripen left, my mother burst into tears. After a while, my father came home with a sullen face and announced that he had tried very hard but not been able to get any money.

My mother said that Nripen had stopped by, looking for him.

My father exploded: 'Shala!' Bastard.

My mother poured water over the burning coals, put out the fire and went to bed.

That story was both funny and sad. I hated my father's selfishness. But looking back with the knowledge of his eventual success, one can lionize his passion and see how that adda in the park with his friends was more important to him than the hunger. Good or bad, that spirit kept him and his friends going, and eventually translated into success for some of them.

His preoccupation with adda never ended. All his life, until he was too old to do so, his living room was never empty. A steady stream of people would walk in unannounced, from early morning until late into the evening. The adda sessions were curtailed a little when he was busy with a production, but they never fully stopped. We always advised him to cut them down and focus more on his work, but he was incapable of and unwilling to change this habit. It remains a mystery to me how he managed to make films, write articles and books and maintain all his professional correspondence while spending most of his waking hours in the company of his friends and, later in his life, his admirers.

Perhaps one way of his dealing with it was by not sleeping much. Even in his younger days, he never slept for more than four or five hours. He would wake up very early, around 4 or 5 in the morning, to get his work done. I remember always waking up to the sound of his portable typewriter. He would sit in front of the west window, overlooking a park, and tap away furiously with two fingers. On every typewriter he owned, the more commonly used keys eventually developed deep indentations in the shape of his fingernails. He never had an administrative assistant, and dealt with all his business correspondence himself. The early mornings were also when he would do his writing, mainly to fulfil some commitment to a magazine. Every morning, there would also always be a single, long phone call with his early-riser friend, Tapas Sen. We could tell he was talking to Sen because he was the only person, other than his brothers, with whom he used the East Bengali dialect.

My father was also the type of personality who performed best under pressure. His entire life was a desperate run to meet some collapsing deadline. I have rarely seen him with a calm composure or in a meditative state of creativity. It was always a frantic rush to finish something. This peculiar mode of thinking came in handy when he had to innovate on his shoots. He rarely followed the script exactly as he wrote it, and kept changing things in the early-morning hours before the shoot or even while taking the shot. This caused considerable difficulty for his film assistants and production team, but it also created a sense of buzz and excitement on his sets.

There was a period in my life when I was working in an orthopaedic research lab in Chicago that specialized in the science of human movement—walking, running, etc. There, I learnt an interesting fact. When we walk, our body is in a stable state. If we're asked to freeze suddenly, we can do so at any moment and hold that position. We cannot do the same while running, because running is never stable. When we run, we initiate a fall with each step but prevent it at the last moment to start another. I always saw my father's life as a run—a long sequence of potential falls that he somehow knew how to prevent, only to initiate another. That was the secret of his creativity.

He was always surrounded by friends, though the nature of the circle changed over time. In the early days, they were all fellow travellers, equals, with similar views, similar ambitions, similar trajectories. Many from that group drifted away over the years, for various reasons. Tapas Sen was the only one who stayed close all through my father's life. Hrishikesh Mukherjee and Salil Chowdhury moved to Bombay and became part of the commercial film world. Though every time they met my father, which was no longer very often, I could still see a spark of the old camaraderie.

Whenever Salil-kaka came home, he and my father would ask each other about common friends from the IPTA days. Sometimes Salil-kaka would sing songs from their activist past. But it was also clear that they lived in different worlds now, that the only common thread was the nostalgia for their time together, when they shared the dreams of a revolutionary future.

My father would sometimes stay with Hrishi-kaka in Bombay. Once, when I was four or five, my father took Ma and me to Bombay, and we all stayed at Hrishi-kaka's Andheri home. Later, Hrishi-kaka's son became a good friend of mine through a shared interest in electronics, and I've stayed quite a few times at their beautiful sea-facing bungalow in Bandra. However, my father and Hrishi-kaka were making different kinds of films, and slowly it was but inevitable that their intellectual lives would drift far apart.

Ritwik-kaka stayed in Calcutta, and though he and my father were both trying to make films with the same objective, another force was pulling them apart—Ritwik-kaka's severe alcoholism. I don't recall ever seeing him sober. No one in my immediate surroundings drank. Therefore, as a child, I was both curious and afraid of drunkenness. Whenever he came to our house, he would be senselessly drunk and abusive, often accompanied by people who could hardly stand straight. I don't recall a day when he and my father had a normal conversation. During my high-school and early college days, on numerous occasions, local boys would knock on our door and report that they'd found Ritwik-kaka lying drunk somewhere. It was then my job to organize a rickshaw to take him home. I was afraid of him if he visited us when my father was not home; he would engage in incoherent and dismissive conversations about my education. Unfortunately, Ritwik-kaka and my father, who could have had the most meaningful conversations, never did so in their later years. They occasionally met, there were casual exchanges of information, but those lacked any kind of depth. The constant veil of an alcohol-induced haze made impossible any meaningful communication.

In the winter of 1976, after many such incidents, Ritwik-kaka was admitted to the hospital for what would be the last time. My father was beside him when he died. His wife, Surama, taught in a school far away, trying to protect her three children from the chaotic life he had created. All of them came to Calcutta and stayed with us until things settled down. It was as if we were one big family. What his addiction took away, it tried to return on his death. When my mother died, I found a tattered letter addressed to her from Surama Ghatak, in which she'd written about the deep bond between the two families. My mother, for some reason, saved the letter in her handbag. I will never understand why we have such romantic notions about extreme addiction among artists. It is nothing but a disease that destroys families, destroys integrity and ultimately destroys humanity.

Even though his earliest circle dissipated over time, my father continued to surround himself with friends. My earliest memories are from the early sixties, when we lived in a tiny two-room ground-floor flat on Manoharpukur Road. The living room was small, almost entirely occupied by a sofa bed and a few low cane stools or moras. And by visitors who came to my father throughout the day, friends as well as coworkers from his latest production. The friend circle in those days comprised people connected with the film-society movement, writers, family friends and artists. As far as I remember, the topics of their conversation spanned cinema, politics, literature and everyday banter. My father wasn't that successful yet, so there were no fans or admirers.

That changed after his success in the late sixties and early seventies. I was older by then, and since that small living room was also where I was supposed to study, I became a silent participant in those conversations. There was a growing group of visitors who admired his work. Some were genuine well-wishers, but an increasing number hoped to benefit from the alliance or simply enjoyed belonging to a polarized camp. I am not sure my father could distinguish these factions as easily as I can today, in hindsight. Praise can be a potent tool to blunt one's ability to judge the real intent of people.

Bengalis have a strange propensity to split any position into two opposite camps. Be it the support for a football team or the way a particular dish should be cooked or how a song should be sung, we indulge in strictly binary choices. If you belong to one side, you must oppose the other with all fury. The same thing happened then: people would champion my father while being unnecessarily critical of Satyajit Ray, with the reverse happening in Ray's circle. A few people had access to both households, and they carried the conversations from one living room to another. They enjoyed the reactions they provoked. I think both Ray and my father were very respectful of each other, but this poisonous atmosphere did stain their thinking. Such is the power of sycophancy.

In my college days, when I began to love challenging my father on any subject I could think of, I remember having many conversations regarding his circle of friends. I would challenge him to name ten friends with whom the intellectual benefit was mutual. I asked him how none of his friends could present any strong opposition to his views. I could see that most of his company was intellectually inferior to him, and while they may benefit from the association, the exchanges were often not reciprocal. I think my father understood this, but was unwilling to accept it. Perhaps that is why he was so eager to attend as many international film festivals as possible, and visit as many college campuses as he could. There, he could spend time talking to those who were his intellectual equals, to those who were interested in his views without being fans or detractors. The honesty of those interactions was essential to his growth, and that honesty was not necessarily being given to him it in his immediate circle.

Towards the end of his life, during the last couple of decades, his friend circle dissipated, but a tiny group of people still visited at a regular cadence. By then, he was also losing his mental ability to engage in stimulating conversations. There were flashes of profound insight, but often he would listen silently. As someone he liked would walk in, his eyes would light up. It was hard for us to watch a man sitting alone when not too long ago, his living room was never empty. The first round of tea used to be served around six in the morning, and the last around eleven at night.

Ironically, when he had the least time to spare, he was surrounded by visitors, but when he had all the time in the world, there was no one to talk to.

MY BONDHU

No one remembers when and why I started calling my father Bondhu. It was a strange way to address a father, as the word means 'friend' in Bengali, my first language. The most likely explanation was that, playing with me one day, he might have said that the two of us were friends, and somehow that got stuck in my mind. Whatever the reason, that is the only name I remember calling him.

This did not create any problems in my early childhood. However, as I got older, I became very self-conscious about such an odd name for my father, and yet I cannot explain why I could not switch to the more acceptable Baba or something similar. When I was eight or nine, I used to study at a school called South Point. The school bus would transport me to and fro. One day, for some reason, my father had to pick me up early. I had to go to the school office to ask for official permission to leave before time. I was asked whether someone had come to pick me up. I said, 'Yes.' They said, 'Who?' And at once I was in a crisis—I could not say Bondhu, yet uttering the word Baba was even harder. So, after much soul searching, I said, 'Ekjon lok.'—A man. Luckily, that was enough for the office to let me go.

Fortunately, in my day-to-day existence as a child, I did not have to call out to him in front of my friends. By then I could manage to refer to him as 'Baba' in conversations with other people, so my secret remained well protected. But there was one incident, from when I was about ten, that still remains with me: one day after Saraswati Puja, when thousands of clay idols are taken to the riverfront in the evening and immersed in the water, my father offered to take my friends and me to watch the spectacle. He was shooting a film then, and the production team had a rented van that could fit us all. This was very exciting for us, since no one had witnessed the immersion ceremony from such close quarters. We all piled into the van, sitting on the bench seats around the edge, and set off.

The immersion ceremony exceeded our expectations—we watched hundreds of Saraswati idols being carried into the water and then let go. After that, my father took us to a narrow lane next to Metro cinema, full of vendors selling various kinds of street food. One shop was selling kulfi ice-cream. My father offered to buy us all a kulfi each. A man brought the ice-creams to us. My father stepped out to pay, and instructed us not to get out of the van while he was away. Suddenly a friend asked me if he could get a glass of water. The responsibility automatically fell upon me to call my father and convey the request.

Now I was in a fix. My father was far away, in front of the kulfi shop, and I was not supposed to get out of the van. I was in a crisis again, and my young brain tried to find a solution where I could snag my father's attention despite the general din and still protect my well-guarded secret nickname for him. Finally, I shouted, 'Mrinal-da!'—using the suffix to indicate older brother, and not realizing how absurd it must have sounded to my friends!

As I grew older, I was no longer afraid to be different and could refer to him as Bondhu in public. One day, during my high-school days, I watched Ray's *Apur Sansar* for the first time. Towards the end of the film, when Apu (played by Soumitra Chatterjee) finally reunites with his little son Kajal, his son asks, 'Who are you?' and the bearded Apu answers, 'Your bondhu.' That was a beautiful confirmation for me.

As my circle expanded in college, my friends spent a good part of the day at our place. My father convinced them to call him 'Mrinal-da', as he was too reluctant to be addressed as kaka or a jetha (uncle). Since then, all my friends have referred to him as Mrinal-da, as has the rest of the world. A couple of my girlfriends have also addressed him as Bondhu, including Nisha, the person I would eventually marry, and her sister Jagriti. There was no need for Nisha to call him anything when we were simply school friends; but after we became a couple, she started calling him Bondhu too.

The relationship between my father and me was rarely like that of a father and son. As a child, I considered him a little too aloof and irresponsible to deserve that role. I never took him too seriously and was convinced he was a bit of an oddball. My uncle Anup Kumar was the male figure in my young life who much better fit the role of father. We mostly lived under the same roof, and he did everything a father was expected to do. He pampered me, spent an enormous amount of time with me and seemed like the person in charge. I used to call him 'Anu', using the nickname by which my parents addressed him. This was also a bit embarrassing, since in our culture one is not supposed to call adults by their name alone but to add some kind of familial suffix.

It was during my high-school days that my relationship with my father began to change. I was growing beyond the world of childish gossip, play and sports, and was discovering the excitement of the intellectual world. I started taking a keen interest in science and the arts. I started having friends with whom I could share my interests in painting, theatre, science, literature, politics. I began to visit art galleries and film-society screenings. I am not sure how much I understood in those days, but that world offered a charm that I found irresistible. Gradually, I found my father more interesting than I had before. I started to understand him and was charmed by his intellect and conversations. He was also gaining a national and international reputation, so I probably also enjoyed his newly found celebrity status.

During my college days and later, our relationship to change. We were genuinely becoming friends. He started to trust my opinions. Not that we always agreed, but there was a deep mutual trust in our sincerity. He knew that if I was critical of some idea or action, then it was worth paying attention. With his growing fame, my father was increasingly surrounded by fans and people who wanted to use their relationship with him for some kind of benefit. I think he enjoyed it all to some extent but was also aware of its limitations. He wanted to be challenged and contradicted, but very few people around him did so. I think this intellectual loneliness is the shared experience of any eminent person in our society. My father appreciated my perspectives, since I never hesitated to challenge him. A psychologist may see the shadow of the eternal struggle between a father and a son—I can neither confirm nor deny that.

There's another reason why I ended up being so critical, which became most apparent whenever he screened a new film for the first time for his friends. It would also be the first time for me. I would be very eager, but also conflicted—while I wanted to watch the film purely from my perspective, I could not stop myself from seeing it from the imagined perspective of the audience at large. I wanted them to like it, and therefore tried to see it from their point of view. When I tried that, I was naturally more concerned about aspects they could potentially dislike. Consequently, I would have many questions and criticisms and fewer positive things to say at the end.

Once everyone was gone and we were back in our private space, my father would ask for my impressions. It would be hard—I wanted to say only good things, but my head would be full of doubts and questions. I knew I had to be honest and open, but I also knew that my father needed support through some positive feedback. It is a nerve-wracking experience for any creative artist to face the audience with new work, and it is even harder for film-makers since one can make only so many films in a lifetime. In that moment of truth, he must have needed more supportive words from his own family, but my mother and I were always brutal.

No matter how painful it was at that moment, my father knew our opinions were more sincere and probably correct. In time, as the newness of the film faded away over the following days, he would engage more with our initial criticisms. I would watch the film several more times over the next several weeks, until I could finally watch it through my own eyes and arrive at my own reactions. This process generally reduced my doubts about a film, and I would have a kinder opinion. In the following weeks and months, I would tell him what I liked, and that always made him very happy.

Over the years, as I matured, the quality of the interactions between us improved significantly. I feel incredibly fortunate to have a friend of his intellect, sensitivity and creativity. I think his gain must have been a bit asymmetric. Still, irrespective of what I could give him, he was grateful for what he received from my mother and me, mainly with regard to our honesty.

It is a pity that the intellectual atmosphere in Calcutta did not allow people of similar intellectual calibres and interests to interact more. There was no shortage of such people in the city, but the cultural atmosphere favoured the formation of small parochial groups who rarely spoke to each other. The likelihood of getting any meaningful feedback diminishes with one's stature. The more famous you get, the less likely you are to receive any helpful criticism. The extraordinary friend circle he had in his formative years had dispersed, but each of them could have benefited if they had remained in close contact.

That was also the story of all his creative friends. There were theatre people like Sombhu Mitra, Utpal Dutt and Ajitesh Bandyopadhyay, all living and working in the same city, yet they rarely spoke to each other. Any time anyone in any group showed any sign of talent, it would inevitably cause a rift, and soon, in Bengali binary fashion, there would be two independent theatre groups where there had been one. There were at least a dozen major writers in the city, but each stayed in their little bubble. The same was true for the visual artists. There was no culture of creative debate, only interpersonal rivalry and polarization.

My friendship with my father evolved with time and probably got deeper after I moved away from Calcutta. We spoke less frequently and met even less. During one phase, when I got him a fax machine, he made a habit of sending me faxes of his writings, newspaper clippings, short notes. When he finally adopted email, we could exchange our thoughts more carefully and deliberately, and also more quickly. However, one thing that changed was how and when I could interact with his films. Gone were the days when I could offer feedback even before the film was made. Gone were the days when I could watch a film when it was screened for the first time. I would only get second-hand reports from my parents. Then, many weeks and months later, I would receive a VHS tape in Chicago and watch it alone. There were things that I liked and things that I didn't, but I no longer felt like I was part of the process. I was just a remote viewer with no impact on the final product. It is perhaps my ego talking, but I could see places in his later films where I would have tried to make a difference.

He wrote a couple of books after he stopped making films in the early years of this century. The first was a memoir titled *Always Being Born*, and later, a very personal view of Charlie Chaplin titled *My Chaplin*. These were both written when he was already using email, which made it much easier for us to exchange notes.

Towards the very end, when his mind was no longer entirely there, I visited them every three months. He did not talk much, but I could see he liked my presence. It was partly because he felt more relieved to see me at his side. He could not help my sick mother any more but felt responsible for her well-being. I could give him a temporary reprieve. He would ask me about my work, my recently acquired interest in making art and the books I read. But his mind was no longer ready to grasp everything; his eyes would drift away, and I would stop talking. What he liked most was to hear about my little successes. I rarely shared such things, but whenever I did, he would say in tones of mock complaint, 'Why don't you tell me these things?'

MY MA

It is impossible to understand my father without the story of my mother, and it is impossible to understand my mother without the story of her beginning.

She was the eldest daughter of three, with a sister a couple of years younger and a brother separated by another couple of years. They grew up in Uttarpara, a small suburb north of Calcutta, which was more of a rural district in those days than a town. Her mother had probably been in her late teens when she was born, and her father in his early twenties.

My maternal grandfather was involved in India's freedom struggle and an active member of the Indian National Congress, arrested for his political activities before he was even thirty. This plunged the family into deep poverty. The extended family tried to help with a little money and food. But, as is always the case, the alms soon dwindled, for the donors themselves were struggling to survive. So, at the young age of fifteen, my mother was forced to become the head of the household. One may question why her mother was not the obvious choice. But the reality of an uneducated woman in her late twenties in the rural India of the forties did not allow for that possibility. My grandmother was not a strong person who could break the rules and do something unconventional. So she succumbed to running the kitchen and the household—but the money had to come from somewhere else.

In the early forties, the Second World War was casting its shadow, even in rural Bengal. The British started creating first-aid posts everywhere, and my mother got a job as a nursing assistant in the local unit. I am not sure how much they paid, but it was certainly not enough to run a family of four.

Eventually, when her father was thirty-two, the British authorities decided to release him as he was suffering from some acute illness, perhaps tuberculosis. The British strategy was to release severely ill inmates since they didn't want to be blamed for a prisoner's death. By the time he was sent home, his illness was quite severe. I am not sure if treatment could have saved his life, but the family didn't have the means to organize any and, over the next few weeks, simply watched him die.

My mother told me that, before his death, he'd once expressed the desire for the popular Bengali sweet called rasogolla. She did not have the money to buy one; he died soon after. Thus, I have never seen my mother eat a rasogolla. I did not share her guilt and regret, but perhaps out of my love for my mother, I have avoided that treat all my life; I don't think I could ever enjoy the taste.

After her father's death, the poverty they were experiencing acquired a permanent status. They could no longer hope that my grandfather would return one day and take responsibility, and things would improve. My mother had to accept the role of being the head of the household for the foreseeable future.

I am still unsure how my mother managed to make ends meet and sustain the family. I am sure they had to depend heavily on other people's kindness, and that created a lifelong trait in my mother to accommodate and tolerate and please others. But along with that, there was a deep sense of resilience, anger and sadness that always lurked behind her apparent calmness. It was this reserve that she would dip into while acting. Before any emotionally demanding scene, she would isolate herself for a few minutes, deep in thought. When I asked her one day if she was thinking about the role or the scene, she said yes she was but she was also thinking about her past. There were painful and complex memories that formed her wealth of emotions from which she tried to summon whatever she needed for the role.

The events in her life between her father's death and her marrying my father are not clearly known to me. She would talk about many incidents, but I cannot arrange them along a consistent timeline. It is a mystery why I didn't ask her more about those days. Her mind was reasonably functional until the end, so I could have asked all the right questions, even until 2016, just a year before her death, to stitch together all her anecdotes into a linear story, but for some reason I did not. Now that she is gone, along with all her contemporaries, we will never be able to clear it up.

I know she went into acting to earn. The film industry was not a wholesome place for young girls in those days. Coming from a small town, she was doubly nervous. This was when she grew close to the family of Dhiren Das, a relative. Das was a well-established playback singer, and a film and theatre actor. He had a large family, and his second son was my uncle Anu, who eventually became a popular film actor and a very important person in my life. My mother partly moved into their large family so Das could offer her the guidance and protection she needed.

As I've mentioned before, she was involved in an activist theatre group called Natya Chakra, a satellite organization of the leftist IPTA. While staging revolutionary plays in remote villages, she came to know personalities such as Bijon Bhattacharya, Ritwik Ghatak, Tapas Sen and my father. She would tell many stories about that phase, clearly a memorable and formative part of her young life. In the year of our country's independence, Bijon Bhattacharya married the writer Mahasweta Devi, Ritwik-kaka's niece. It was a small and close-knit group.

I also heard stories of her association with my father. She was cast in a major role in a film called *Du Dhara*, of which my father was the writer. During the shooting, he would often accompany her back home to Uttarpara, sometimes even walking the whole way to save on bus and train fares. This was apparently when they started to form a romantic relationship.

Again, I cannot organize these events along a linear timeline. Was her association with Natya Chakra before or after *Du Dhara*? Did she meet my father while shooting this film and then come to know his common friends? Was she living with Das' extended family before she acted in *Du Dhara* or after? These are simple questions that I could have asked her any time I wanted, but I did not. Perhaps someone with a historian's perspective can still try to connect the dots, but I doubt it, since all the sources are now dead. It is surprising how fragile our memories are. Life stories do not last more than a generation. If we don't capture them at the right time, they are lost forever. Ordinary people, whose only influence is limited to their immediate family and friends, lose all their stories within a generation. My mother had a little more fame than most of us, yet her stories have been destroyed by the ravages of time. All we can see now are the broken shards of glass, not the whole.

My mother loved telling stories. Many of them were from her childhood, before all the extreme hardships. Stories of the small, rural town that Uttarpara used to be. It is these stories that created my impression of small-town, rural life in India in the thirties and forties. Later in my childhood, I spent a lot of my time in Uttarpara. The place had not changed much between my mother's childhood and mine. The cast of characters were still there, only a couple of decades older. These were stories of pain and suffering, of nobility and sacrifice, of loss and survival, all located in a small town by the river. What I am today, living halfway around the globe, is the sum of all those stories.

She also had very fond memories of her IPTA days. This was when she came to know several of the intellectuals from the city, who opened up a larger world for a girl who'd had to stop her education at the age of twelve. She would tell me about a day when she walked for hours to get from central Calcutta to Uttarpara while Ritwik-kaka—before he was a filmmaker—narrated to her the story of Joan of Arc. She told me about how they were threatened for their leftist plays by rival political groups, but still dared to stage them in remote villages. She was proud of her role in a play called *Neel Darpan*, directed by Bijon Bhattacharya. There were stories of travelling with shadow plays—a white cloth would be hoisted in a field after dark, and my father and others would paddle a bicycle on bricks to power the small dynamo that in turn powered a small light. Tapas Sen and his team members would use paper cutouts placed between the light and the screen to cast shadows and enact a shadow play.

However, she rarely talked about the hardships. She did not say much about how she ran her family. They had very little, and simply surviving was enormously difficult. They often starved, and that caused her to develop chronic illnesses. She was exceedingly thin, and at some point was so sick that she had to be admitted to the School of Tropical Medicine for diagnosis and long-term treatment. I am sure that government-run hospital was no paradise, yet from my mother's stories, it sounded like one. She spent three months there and gained some weight. The square meals at the hospital did the trick, and she often talked about that experience as many of us would talk about a long holiday.

Her lack of formal education remained a sore point all her life. She loved reading Bengali novels but learning English proved to be tough. When my father started expanding his horizons beyond Calcutta, the lack of English-language skills became an issue. In 1966, we bought our first record player. It was a simple blue model called 'Star' manufactured by HMV. It had to be connected to our Murphy radio through a thin cable, and the sound came out of the radio. My father purchased two Rabindrasangeet LP albums, and they remained the only two records we possessed for many years.

A year later, my father ordered a box full of 45 rpm records called the Linguaphone. It was a set of records and books that formed a spoken-English teaching course. The intention was to teach my mother to speak English. Soon, this became a contentious issue in our household. My mother's enthusiasm was sporadic. She would use it for a couple of days and then shelve it. This frustrated my father; he would pester her to practise and often remind her that the course was not all that inexpensive. This effort did not work, and finally, at some point, the box of records was moved out of sight.

As my father got exposed to the national scene, more and more people from elsewhere in the country would visit. Their conversations were always in English, and my mother could not participate. In India, an inability to speak English is often indistinguishable from being uneducated. My father tried to avoid embarrassing situations, and my mother felt underconfident and tried her best to stay away from any such interactions.

The situation got worse when my father started to get invited to international film festivals, and my mother was invited with him. Now she could no longer hide in the bedroom. However, two things happened simultaneously. She quickly realized that outside India, especially in Europe and Asia, a lack of English was not viewed as a sign of being uneducated. Many people attending these festivals, most of whom were well-known and well-respected individuals, also did not speak English. Therefore, my mother no longer felt all that awkward speaking in her broken English, and my father also relaxed a little. Second, she started acting in my father's films again and quickly gained a reputation for being a fine actor, both in India and abroad. Her identity was no longer defined as my father's wife but as an actor with significant talent.

More than her lack of English, she acutely felt the lack of the basic knowledge one acquired through formal education, and was embarrassed by it. I remember the first time she travelled outside India. It was in 1972, right after I finished high school. My father was invited to head the jury at the Mannheim Film Festival in Germany, and he wanted me and my mother to join him. It was the first international trip for both of us. At one point during the flight, we could see the peaks of the Alps poking out through dense clouds. As we enjoyed this magnificent sight, my mother suddenly said with genuine amazement that she did not know there were mountains in the sky. She was deeply embarrassed when we started laughing, and immediately understood her mistake. These were the moments when I could see a profound regret in her eyes at not having had the opportunity to learn what everyone seems to at school and college. She was very self-conscious too that she would make similar mistakes in front of other people.

During the second half of her life, she travelled the world with my father. Every time she would see something new and exotic, my father would tease her by uttering a single word: 'Bhadrakali', the name of the post office in Uttarpara where she grew up. It is probably true that my mother was the only representative of that time and place to visit these exotic locations, and she always felt exceptionally fortunate for that turn of events.

My father was, in every respect, a very disorganized person. He had no ability to take care of his everyday needs and depended entirely on my mother. He did not know how to cook, do laundry, iron his clothes, pack his bags or even keep track of his medicines. Of course, he could have done all of this, but it was convenient for him to pretend complete incompetence and rely on my mother to fill the gap.

This reminds me of another story. When my father was in his sixties, he was attending a film festival in Europe. My mother was not with him. He had to go from one city to another, and a young woman, perhaps an admirer, was to drive him over. The drive was a few hours long, and the two spent the time in long conversations. When he reached his destination, he went to his hotel room to freshen up; he was supposed to meet the woman again for dinner. My father said that he felt a tinge of excitement as he was preparing for the evening. After a shower, he put on a starched and newly pressed white kurta. At which point he realized a critical button was missing. He was getting late for his rendezvous, so he hurriedly looked for another kurta. As he was rummaging through his suitcase, which, as usual, had been organized by my mother, he suddenly discovered a small plastic bag at the bottom containing a few emergency essentials. Through the transparent plastic, he could see a threaded sewing needle that my mother had put in for just such an emergency.

He later told us that the slight spark of romantic excitement that had flared up in him vanished instantly.

Did he ever have any romantic association with any other woman? I have never heard or felt anything indicating that. Neither have I heard of such rumours, which are easy to spread in the case of celebrities. So, even if he ever felt differently, which we will never know, he must have restrained himself from acting on the impulse.

True, my mother did not have any formal education beyond primary school. Yet, she was exceptionally dignified. interacting with her would probably never guess that she lacked formal education. I often wonder where that came from. She grew up in a rural setting, and her milieu lacked sophistication. When I place her next to all her friends and relatives from her hometown, she stands out as an obvious outsider. Perhaps what changed her was her exposure to a much larger world. First, through her theatre friends, and later, through my father's ever-expanding circle that finally enclosed every corner of the world. There was also, no doubt, an innate sophistication in her that helped her climb out of her rustic background.

We lived in a culture where education was of paramount importance. The intelligentsia in India is acutely focused on knowledge and scholarship. Yet, I have always noticed the expression of genuine respect that everyone in our friend circle showed towards her. This is partly due to her acting skills and her overall dignity. I believe it was also due to the respect that my father had for her. Any lengthy conversation with my father would inevitably make this evident, and that allowed people to look beyond her lack of formal education and appreciate her emotional intelligence and wisdom.

It may be a bit silly for a son to appreciate the beauty of a mother, because everyone believes their mother to be beautiful, but I can't resist sharing my opinion. I believe she had a rare kind of beauty that combined infinite kindness with a deep, hidden sadness, as if there was a storm always brewing under her calm exterior. She was as strong as a tree trunk that could withstand the toughest storms.

She was a complex and beautiful human being.

OUR HOMES

Since my birth, we have lived in five different buildings. My parents got married when my father was without a job and penniless. He lived with his parents and brothers in a flat in Park Circus. That is where my grandfather, a well-known lawyer in Faridpur, set up home after fleeing East Bengal after the Partition. My father had moved to Calcutta earlier as a student and lived in rented rooms or a 'mess', a boarding house. However, when the rest of his family moved to Calcutta, he moved in with them. They were in a difficult financial situation, somehow managing to survive. His elder brothers had a meagre income that went towards supporting the household, but my father was unemployed. He had quit his medical-representative job and was fruitlessly pursuing his passion for becoming a filmmaker.

I am not exactly sure why they decided to get married at that point. My mother's financial situation was worse, so perhaps there was a desire to 'rescue' her. If that was the intent, it certainly didn't work. My mother was still responsible for her mother and two younger siblings. After she moved in with my father's family, my grandparents welcomed and loved her. Still, there was apparent resentment from some of his other brothers who were struggling to make ends meet and had to worry about their own families. In that atmosphere, my mother suffered emotionally for being married to the most irresponsible and useless family member.

My mother moved in right after they got married, at a very small event with a handful of close friends and a plate of chanachur as refreshment. As was the tradition, my mother attended the wedding ceremony barefoot. The next day, she realized she could not leave the house as she did not have a pair of sandals. Soon after that, my father asked for the only jewellery she had received from his parents so that he could pawn it and pay his share of the house-hold expenses. Pawning was a one-way street for him, and she never saw her bangles again.

A year later, when my father somehow managed to get the chance to direct his first film, he used that slight financial security to move out of my grandfather's home and rent a place—a single room on the top floor of a three-storey building on Ashwini Dutta Road. By then my mother was pregnant.

As the day of her delivery drew near, she moved to Uttarpara to be with her mother and two siblings; my father was busy shooting *Raat Bhore*. When her labour pains began, her cousin brought her to a small private nursing home in South Calcutta. Citizen's Nursing Home on Hazra Road, owned by a doctor close to the Communist Party, who knew my father and wanted to help. My father had been shooting through the night before and came home early in the morning for a quick nap. When he woke up in the afternoon, he rushed to see my mother. By the time he got to her, she was resting. Hearing his clothes rustle beside her, my mother opened her eyes. My father asked, 'Have they said when?' My mother turned away: 'It's already happened.'

My father had slept through my birth!

They were utterly unprepared to welcome a baby home. Someone gave them a little pillow for me to lie on. They rolled some old newspapers into bolsters, so I would not roll over. My mother was too thin and frail to produce adequate breast milk, so the nursing home started them off with a pack of a baby formula called Similac. The bottle broke on the trip back home. My parents could not replace it, and my only chance to enjoy a sip of formula preparation was lost forever. I survived on my mother's short supply.

On a side note, the film that made my father inadvertently ignore the birth of his only son was an utter failure. Never again, until his death, have I been able to make him talk about it. He simply wanted to wash it away from his memory. Any mention of it, and he would utter just one disgusted word—baaje—terrible. Only through other sources did I one day come to know that it had starred the powerful matinee idol, Uttam Kumar.

After about two years in the rooftop flat, my parents started looking to move into a slightly larger place with a separate bedroom and a small kitchen. They found it, but the homeowners were reluctant to rent it to a family from East Bengal. In those days, refugees from the East were not considered desirable tenants. However, this problem was overcome when they realized that my mother was from West Bengal, and that my uncle, the actor Anup Kumar, was willing to stand as a guarantor of sorts.

When we moved into the Manoharpukur Road flat, I was just one year and ten months old. The homeowners lived upstairs— parents and five children, aged between ten and twenty—while we occupied a part of the ground floor. I became a big hit with the brothers and sisters, and we lived like a large extended family. Growing up, many of my meals were eaten at their place and the children were like my older siblings.

The house was in a narrow lane off the main street that ended in a slum. Because of its peripheral location, we had a strange street address: 22/1/1/21 Manoharpukur Road. The too many unnecessary slashes in the address perhaps bothered my father's aesthetic sense, so he started using a slightly shorter version: 22/1/21. We never missed any mail because of this abbreviation, so I guess he was correct. The road meandered a little with about a dozen buildings before it reached the slums. Since there was no way to drive through and no easy way to turn around, the taxis refused to enter our street, citing the most unlikely explanation that driving a taxi in reverse gear would destroy the fare meter. Most of the houses had middle-class residents, and very few had cars. As a result, the street was mostly quiet, with little to no traffic.

Around 1965, the actor Soumitra Chatterjee moved into our street. Our two families grew very close during those years. My uncle was a good friend of his, and he had acted in quite a few of my father's films too. My mother was a friend of his wife, Deepa, a prize-winning badminton player and a lively personality. They had an interior decorator do up their flat before they moved in, and it was the first time I saw a home decorated with contemporary aesthetics. Around that time, he also bought a white Ambassador car, and that was another first time for me—the sight of a car straight out of the showroom. I remember the excitement of riding in it once when my uncle had borrowed it. Eventually, they moved to a larger space on Purna Das Road, and the regular contact between the two families faded away.

Towards the end of 1968 or in early 1969, the film industry in West Bengal was torn into two combating factions. I no longer recall the exact political differences, but the polarization was fierce. On one side was the more left-leaning faction that included one of the two actors' organizations, Abhinetry Sangha, led by Soumitra Chatterjee and assisted by my uncle Anup Kumar. This faction also included the leftist technicians and directors, including my father. The other side had the slightly conservative actors' guild, Shilpi Sangsad, led by Uttam Kumar. Most of the financiers of the film industry were on the conservative side, and they began to blacklist those on the left of the divide.

Our little living room became the headquarters of the leftist faction. It was a tremendously exciting time for me. Even though I did not understand much of it, I loved the huge crowd that congregated from early in the morning, and sometimes even spilt over into the street. There were heated conversations throughout the day. The daily visitors included many important actors of the time, so the balconies of all the houses around us served as day-long galleries. Friends and relatives of the neighbours would come over and take permanent seats at the verandas and windows, just to get a glimpse of the film stars who came and went. One of the protests centred on the release of Satyajit Ray's *Goopy Gyne Bagha Byne* in May 1969. Even though Ray stayed away from either side of the divide, some conflict between the producers and theatre owners crystallized around its release. The successful release was seen as a victory for the left, but both sides were probably quite tired of fighting. After that, the tensions slowly faded away, and the blacklisting of the actors on the left was gradually forgotten.

During those years, most of my friends were children from the neighbourhood slums. This was perfectly fine during my younger years when friendships are generally formed around play. However, as I grew older, my interests began to drift in different directions. A gap began to appear in our friendships, as I could no longer find much intellectual resonance with them. Yet, I couldn't pull myself away from them either. So, when we decided to move to a slightly larger flat on a nearby street, I was in a way relieved—it gave me an excuse to change my circle without explicitly betraying my childhood bonds.

In the middle of 1969, we moved a few streets to the south, to Motilal Nehru Road. This was a larger one-bedroom flat, more cheerful, with windows that let in plenty of daylight. It was on the second floor of a building, and we could see Deshapriya Park from our living-room window and small balcony. It wasn't an expansive view—our building was not on the main road—but the park was visible as a narrow green strip through two buildings. The east-facing bedroom also got much more daylight, as the next building was only one-storey tall. It even had a dining room, but that was one floor up, built as an add-on structure on the roof. So, finally, we invested in a dining table for the first time. Before this, we'd always eaten sitting on the floor, in the usual Bengali middle-class way. This upward social mobility, however, was not destined to happen. Both the kitchen and the rooftop dining room had a thin asbestos roof, which made the rooms unbearably hot during most of the year. So after trying out the odd routine of locking up our main door, walking up a flight of stairs and then eating like 'civilized' people, we quickly abandoned the idea; the food was carried down to our bedroom, and we resumed the practice of sitting on the floor and eating.

While we lived on Manoharpukur Road, Anu had the strange idea of having a radiogram. In those days, this was the ultimate status symbol: a substantial piece of cupboard-sized wooden furniture that would hold a record player, a radio, an amplifier and racks to store the records. Of course, we did not have the resources to purchase one, so he planned to build one at home. He found a fantastic electronic engineer named Atin Bandyopadhay, who would come to our flat and solder together the electronics. It was before the days of transistors, so this was to be an amplifier made from glass vacuum tubes, or valves, as they were commonly called. However, Atin-babu was less than regular; after working on it for a few days, he would disappear for weeks. In the meantime, my uncle brought in carpenters who set up shop on our neighbour's front porch, building the cabinet for Atin-babu's electronics. Little thought was put into deciding where precisely in our tiny flat that monstrosity would be placed.

The promised piece of electronics was never finished, but it proved to be a turning point in my life—I was mesmerized by Atin-babu's skills. He was not only a great engineer who could start soldering the components without any schematic, except for the design he had in his head, but also an artist. Everything was perfect and visually gorgeous in how he arranged his components and laid out the wires. I was hooked on electronics from that time onwards, and what started as a hobby later became my profession for a while and is now my tool as an artist.

When my uncle gave up on the idea of having a radiogram, the box was modified into a book and curio cabinet for our Motilal Nehru Road flat, and the vertical speakers turned into bookshelves. I kept tinkering with the electronics during my school and college days, and ultimately built our homegrown stereo system, though bereft of the beauty of what Atin-babu could have built. Some people come into our lives for a brief period and get lost forever, never knowing the impact they leave behind on another human being. That makes me ask the unanswerable question: Have I been fortunate enough to be such an agent in someone else's life?

For the first time in our living room, there was a narrow working table. That is where my father did all his typing and writing. When he was not using it, the typewriter would go into a narrow shelf under the table, and the writing desk would transform into my electronic workbench. There was an L-shaped sitting area, which is where we met people. My father's friends and colleagues, but in time also my friends. This was a substantial group of five to ten of us during my college days. When my father had guests, I would move my group into the bedroom. If my uncle had guests, they would move onto the balcony. Essentially, the whole house was always full of people. There was also not much separation between my friends and my father's. In all this excitement, we forgot about my mother's need for privacy. She was only forty-some years old then, still a young woman by many accounts, but we never gave her any space she could call her own. Her bedroom was often filled with my friends, primarily males in their twenties. I will never understand our collective insensitivity and her infinite ability to tolerate it all.

Having moved from an even smaller space, my father must have had a distorted notion of the vastness of our 150-square-foot living room. While shooting *Ichchhapuran* in 1970, a children's film based on the only Tagore story he ever worked with, three young technicians arrived from Bombay: K. K. Mahajan the cinematographer, H. K. Verma assisting Mahajan and Narinder Singh the sound recordist. Instead of putting them up in a hotel, my father asked them to stay with us. At night, the living-room furniture was moved to make room for their makeshift beds. If that was not bad enough, we all had to use the only bathroom in the flat. They had to leave early for the daily shoot, so they had to start getting ready even earlier, to make sure each got his turn. The biggest sufferer was Narinder Singh—a very proper Sikh, always well dressed, he needed considerable time to take care of his long hair and put it all into a well-wrapped turban. By the time he came out of the tiny bathroom, he would be drenched in sweat. So painful was this sight that Anu hung a small ceiling fan in the bathroom. It did not help much, but the gesture was appreciated.

We lived in that flat through one of the most critical phases of my father's career. We moved in when he'd finished making *Bhuvan Shome* in 1969, the film that secured for him both national and international acceptance. And we lived there until 1980, which covered his Calcutta Trilogy, as well as *Chorus* (1974), *Mrigayaa* (1976), *Oka Oorie Katha* (1977), and marked the start of the next phase of more introspective films, such as *Ek Din Pratidin* (1979).

During the last few years at Motilal Nehru Road, another change happened in my personal life—I fell in love with the person

I would eventually marry, Nisha. She and I had been classmates since high school, but that had been a simple friendship. Until we met again while organizing a school reunion. In 1977, the friendship turned into something else, and we started seeing each other regularly.

Calcutta is not a friendly place for young couples seeking a quiet, romantic time. Therefore, we spent our time either at my home or at Nisha's, or walking between my home and New Alipur. Nisha was another claimant in our living room—she often came over after her college classes ended mid-afternoon. My father would then retreat into the bedroom to give us some privacy. But it was torture for him, as his working desk was in the living room. Nisha and I both felt guilty about depriving him of his space, but we didn't have the heart to sacrifice our privacy. Sometimes, when we felt too guilty and had some money to spare, we would spend time at a local Chinese restaurant called Mandarin.

In February 1980, we got married. I was still a student at the Indian Statistical Institute. It is not common for a man to get married without an income, but it did not seem odd to any of us, as we never had a notion of whose money it was in our family. We always felt that there was a single pool for all of us to use as needed. Looking back, I realize getting married was an odd decision to make, but it did not feel so at that time. Until then, I never had a room of my own, but now there was need for one. So the search for a two-bedroom flat began, and one was found further in Bhabanipur: 14 Beltala Road. It was on the second floor of a building and had two small bedrooms, a living room, a small balcony and even a dining space adjoining the kitchen. Plus, for the first time, we had the luxury of two bathrooms. However, we had to forego the pleasure of having an open view as other taller buildings surrounded the house.

As usual, Anu took charge of setting up the new flat, and he could barely finish decorating the first bedroom by the time of the wedding. So, in February, Nisha and I moved into the new flat while the rest of the household stayed back in the old one. Every evening, Nisha and I went over to have our meals with my parents and Anu. Eventually, after a few more weeks, the big move was completed, and we all started to live together under the same roof.

My circle of friends in those days had several young artists, including Abhijit Gupta and Nitish Roy, who both helped design the interior of my and Nisha's bedroom. As a result, that one room looked quite different from the typical middle-class hodge-podge of furniture and artefacts. It seemed rather posh and sophisticated. So whenever anyone important visited my father, he would prefer to take them to our room, both for a bit of privacy and perhaps for the sophistication and aesthetic quality of the space. However, since that room did not have a sitting area, the guest would be given a chair pulled out from the dining room while my father would sit on our bed. Around that time, my father's films developed a demand in Europe, and his European agents, Eliane Stutterheim and Donat Keusch, would visit Calcutta from time to time. Whenever they came, we had to vacate our bedroom for them. I still recall a telegram that we once received from my father when he was in Delhi: ELIANE COMING ARRANGE TOILET PAPER.

Right across our living-room window was an all-girls school. Soon after we moved, the rumour must have spread there that there could be film-star sightings through that window. Even though we rarely had such visitors, just the possibility was enough to excite the teenage girls. During their lunch break, all the barred windows of the school would be crowded with girls, packed like sardines in a can, each jostling to squeeze in and get a glimpse into the world of glamour and fashion. Despite daily failures to see anything worthwhile, the enthusiasm lasted almost a year until the crowd started thinning out and finally disappeared.

That living room became the production office for all the rest of the films my father made. My mother, though, finally had a room with some privacy, since any extra visitors could use the dining room rather than her bedroom, and I could entertain my friends in my and Nisha's bedroom.

My stay in that house did not last that long. After working on my PhD at the Indian Statistical Institute for a year, my advisor moved to a university abroad. So I decided to find an alternative and enrolled in the graduate program at a university in the US. Nisha was also working on her PhD in reproductive biology, but was further ahead in her research. Therefore, in 1983, I left for Chicago while Nisha stayed behind to finish her doctorate. This decision was a big blow to my parents, especially my mother. Like all mothers, she was at once happy and sad. As the day of my departure drew closer, my father gave her an option—he had to go to Toronto around that time for the film festival, and my mother could accompany him. If she agreed, they could leave from Toronto after the festival and arrive in Chicago in time to receive me. But that would mean she wouldn't be able to see me off from Calcutta. She agreed to this arrangement, as it would give her a chance to see for herself what I would call home for the next few years. In autumn 1983, I left home for good—but I did not know that then. Nisha rushed to finish her thesis, and left Calcutta the following spring to join me.

The collective life our family had built over the last three decades was destroyed in a quick blow. Nisha and I came back home often, but it was never the same. Our family was no longer operating as a team. We were each on our own—my father making his films, and I making my life choices. The distance between us became palpable and very real.

My father was often advised to buy a flat rather than live in a rented space. However, since the early seventies, his resources always fell just slightly short of the market price of desirable places. When the flats sold for around a hundred thousand rupees, his resources amounted to about half that value. As prices increased, his savings increased as well, but the two-to-one ratio remained, and he could never buy a flat. There was also a lack of passion from his side, as he was never too excited about the responsibilities of property ownership. Around 2002, our landlords announced that they would not be able to rent the flat any more. His filmmaking career was coming to an end, and he realized his income stream would vanish soon. Thus the security of owning a place finally became real to him, and he started looking to purchase a property. As before, the market price was still twice that of his savings. However, I now had some savings of my own, and we decided to pool our resources and accomplish what we could not do in the past. This was when we purchased a modern fourth-floor flat on Padmapukur Road, and my parents moved one final time.

The move to Padmapukur coincided with my father's retirement from filmmaking. However, unlike retirement from a job, which is done with a certain finality, retirement from a creative life is a fuzzy affair. He never thought that, at the age of eighty, *Amar Bhuvan* would be his last film. He struggled with the concept of making another film, incessantly looked for ideas, developed some detailed treatments, but ultimately backed out. A writer or a painter can continue to produce, perhaps at a smaller scale or frequency, and taper off their creative output. Filmmaking is an expensive endeavour, both in terms of money and energy. Therefore, at some point, there is a sudden stop. One cannot make smaller and smaller films. I often encouraged him to make a set of short films and compile them into a saleable package, but that never happened.

At Padmapukur Road, as his productions stopped, so did the visits from all the work-related people. The steady stream of friends slowed down to a trickle too. Multiple factors caused this. The location was not as central as our previous residence, and people who depended on public transportation found it challenging. His circle of friends was also ageing and had less energy to make the trip. Above all, he was probably losing the energy and charm that had attracted and held together his following. He was no longer an active artist but a filmmaker from the past.

This flat was a much more spacious, with bedrooms for my parents and us, an office-cum-library and a large dining area. My father was pleased with it, and I just wish he could have enjoyed it while he was genuinely active. For example, just having a separate office where he could retreat and focus on his work and where all his books were within easy access would have been such a help. I cannot avoid wondering if a better working environment could have influenced his work. We will never know for sure, but I have a strong suspicion that it could have had a significant impact. We all tend to attribute creativity and an artist's creative output to mysterious powers within us. We rarely ask how mundane physical things can also affect the creative process, both positively and negatively.

My father took full advantage of the better working environment while writing his longer pieces. Before this time, his writing had been confined to screenplays and articles for various publications. Even the books that had been published at the time were compilations of such articles. However, in 2003, he started working on the manuscript of his autobiography, *Always Being Born*. That was the first time he wrote a whole book. That was also when he was finally getting somewhat comfortable with the computer and email. He had been using an electronic typewriter for a while, where he could edit the typed text to some extent, until he switched to a computer. Though he ended up using the computer more or less like an extended typewriter. He would type the text, print it out, make corrections on the printout, then fax them to me. Over time, he became more comfortable using a more comprehensive range of word-processing tools, including cut and paste, though it needed some retraining after even the shortest gap.

When he was working on *Always Being Born*, I observed a significant decline in his mental capacity. Initially, it was very subtle, and only people close to him could sense it. Around 2003, my parents visited us in Chicago because Nisha had just undergone major brain surgery and was in no shape to travel. One evening, he was talking to a couple of my American friends. I wanted my father to be at his conversational best; for obvious reasons, I wanted them to be impressed. But that evening I realized his anecdotes had lost some of their power—the connections he was making were weaker, and the timing less than perfect. It was very subtle, but I told Nisha that evening that Bondhu was getting old.

Over the next few years, his brain continued to slow down. He could no longer gather his thoughts on the fly and had difficulty remembering the names of people and places and in processing his sensory inputs. He would ask me about something, and I could see that I was losing him as I replied. He could manage simple, everyday conversations, but anything complex and conceptual would often stump him.

I think he was realizing his own shortcomings, and therefore writing was his way of battling that decline—he could take his time, think things through, consult reference materials to remind him of the details, and make up for his limitations. We encouraged him to avoid live interviews and respond in writing instead. This was a difficult period for all of us—the person who was an excellent storyteller and liked talking more than anything else was slowly falling silent. Towards the end, he would start a sentence but then suddenly stop, desperately trying to gather his thoughts, but his mind would not cooperate and his face would be marked by his painful frustration.

The Padmapukur flat became a space of increasing gloom. As their health deteriorated, I began to visit more often to take care of things. During the last ten years, I made a trip every three or four months. But every time I was there, I would feel more depressed. There was a constant deluge of problems beyond our ability to completely solve. My parents were mostly confined to their respective beds, only coming to the dining table for their meals. My mother's physical health was worse, but her mental state was better. My father was physically fit—even through a fall and a hip replacement—until a second fall and a second hip replacement. After the first, he was determined to get better and did everything his doctor advised to regain muscular strength. But he gave up after the second and never fully recovered.

During the last few years, my parents hardly spoke because of their health. My mother was bedridden most of the time and lost weight at an alarming rate. My father had a hospital bed, making their bedroom look especially depressing. One day after her third stroke, my mother went into a coma-like state. This led to more hospital equipment coming into the room. Amid the constant whirring sounds of these machines, my mother lived another few months, and then, one afternoon, stopped breathing. My father was lying in his bed next to her.

My mother's death took away the last purpose for him to live, and he slowly gave up fighting. After a year, it was his turn, but fortunately, there was no prolonged suffering. I could not be at his side when he died, but that was all right.

THE LIGHTER SIDE

If we ask someone to draw a personality profile of my father by looking at his creative output alone, it may look something like this: a grave and serious man, thoughtful and intense, perhaps a little angry. However, anyone who knew him closely would probably also mention that he was an exceptionally humorous individual. In fact, many people close to him often remember that aspect of his personality more than anything else.

There is a stark distinction between how we remember a public personality and how we remember a personal acquaintance. For most of us, we are only remembered by our personal friends through a lifetime of interactions. It is somewhat different for celebrities. We know them through their work and their public persona. In that respect, since my father mostly made serious cinema, on somewhat heavy subjects, it is natural that he would be imagined as a very serious person—maybe even a bit grim.

In his private life, he was a person with an unusual sense of humour and an extraordinary ability for self-ridicule. The non-stop addas at our place were not just fuelled by passionate political debates or deep discussions on aesthetics, but also by laughter you could hear around the block, and at the centre of it all that was my father. He always had an endless collection of funny anecdotes to share, was always ready to pull someone's leg, to see something funny in the gravest of matters and never hesitated to make fun of himself.

There are too many stories to tell, but let me pick a few from various times in his life—some from even before I was born.

There are many stories he liked to tell about his childhood in the small town of Faridpur, now in Bangladesh. A common thread that ran through all of them his general cowardice in the face of physical danger. When he was a teenager, a few burglaries occurred in their neighbourhood. As a reaction, the residents decided to create what was called a civil-protection team. All the young people were automatically recruited, and were to take turns to be vigilant during the night. If they saw anything unusual, they were supposed to raise the alarm. Eventually, it was my father's turn. He went to bed but tried to stay alert with his weapon of choice, a well-oiled narrow bamboo pole next to his bed.

In the middle of one night, a neighbour raised the alarm. My father sat up, picked up his weapon and stepped out. What he didn't expect was to see a man running away down the street. He instantly gave chase. After a few turns down the street, the burglar suddenly stopped, spun around and looked straight at my father—who was still running towards him with his bamboo pole, ready to strike—and uttered a loud bark. In an instant, my father's resolve and bravery vanished. He swiftly turned around and began to run back home at a greater speed than he had pursued his target. When he finally met a group of neighbours, all armed with poles, they asked him if he had seen the burglar; he said he had been looking, but hadn't seen a thing.

Many years later, just after my parents were married and had moved into the rooftop room, one night, they heard the landlord and other neighbours shouting from the street below. My mother went to the window to be able to better listen. They were asking my father to open the stairwell door, for they suspected a thief may have somehow entered the building. As with many old buildings in the city, there was a metal gate at the street-level entrance to the stairwell. That gate was locked at night, and unlocked every morning. Since our family was the last to go to bed, it was my father who usually performed that task. Bondhu got out of bed and began to tie his dhoti, so that he could rush downstairs and unlock the gate. The neighbours were getting impatient, they kept asking him to come down with the keys. My father, though, kept struggling with his dhoti knot, which proved to be an extraordinarily complicated task that night. At some point, my mother's patience ran out—she asked for the keys so that she could go down herself. This infuriated my father, and he screamed at her and told her to shut up. Finally, he came up with a safer solution and simply dropped the keys from their window to the pavement below. When they finally heard many voices outside the room, only then could my father finish tying the knot on his dhoti and open the door and meet the rest of the investigative team.

When I was a little boy, I was made to drink a glass of milk every morning. Given our financial situation, milk was a precious commodity. One morning, our helper boy, Prasanna, was warming the milk for me while my father was shaving at another end of the room, using a small mirror on the wall. In that mirror, he could clearly see the kitchen. As he shaved, he watched Prasanna pour the warm milk into a cup, add sugar, and then, instead of bringing the cup to me, continued to take unhurried sips. My father was in a quandary—he told us later that he didn't want to turn around and face Prasanna after what he had just seen. Yet he was already done with his shaving. Having no choice, he picked up his shaving brush and lathered himself all over again.

Anu once told me about an incident from the very early days of my father's filmmaking career. Anu and my father were in a taxi.

My father was excitedly talking about something. As usual, he had a cigarette between his fingers. At one point, he discarded the burning stub down the hole in the backrest of the front seat. Usually, in most cars of that time, that was where the ashtray used to sit. But many taxi operators would remove that ashtray to discourage passengers from smoking in the car. This was one such taxi; but my father was so engrossed in his conversation that he'd failed to notice the absence of the metallic tray.

My uncle did notice it and shouted, 'What have you done? The stuffing inside the backrest will catch fire!' My father immediately realized the magnitude of his mistake and said, 'Let's get off!' My uncle was more sensible and asked the taxi to stop in front of a paan shop. He got off, bought a bottle of soda water, got back into the cab and poured the soda down the hole in the backrest. By then, the taxi driver had realized what was going on and was shouting out all the obscenities he had in stock. My uncle dropped the fare and a generous tip on the seat, and he and my father slowly walked away before a crowd gathered.

But not all the anecdotes are about him and his timidity or fear. My mother used to narrate a story from when I was four or five years old. Of course, I don't remember it. It seems that when I was a child, I loved eating sandesh, a popular sweet in Bengal. However, my parents could not afford to buy them for everyone at home; they would often buy one just for me. One day, as I was eating my favourite sweet with clumsy hands, small crumbs of it fell on the ground. Bondhu started picking up the crumbs and eating them. This apparently caused a painful dilemma for me—I did not have the heart to share my sweet with him, but I also felt guilty at ignoring his obvious desire for a piece. I started to cry, complaining about my father eating the scattered crumbs.

Many of the anecdotes my father repeated frequently are not particularly flattering. They all relate to some perceived shortcoming
of his—his appearance, his abilities or his work.

Right after their unceremonious wedding, he was visiting his
shoshur-bari, his in-laws', in Uttarpara. As he walked down a
narrow lane, an elderly fellow stopped him. 'Did you marry Gita?'
he asked. My father sheepishly nodded. The man peered at my
father's face very intently, as if looking for something, and declared,
'Kalo, kintu oto kalo to noy'—He's dark, but not so dark either.
My father may have blushed, but it was lost on his not-so-dark
complexion.

A year later, I was born. When I was four, all of us went to
Bombay. My father's close friend, Hrishikesh Mukherjee, who had
already established himself as a successful film director, lived
in Bombay, and all three of us put up at Hrishi-kaka's Andheri
bungalow. He had two children—Babu, who was a couple of years
older than me, and Tutul, who was my age.

One evening they had some guests over, including a well-
known female actor. Every man in the room, my father included,
was trying to be as presentable as possible in the company of that
young and beautiful woman.

At some point, Tutul, the younger son, came over to my father
and sat on his lap. This, from my father's perspective, was a welcome
development—it gave him more visibility. In a room full of grown-
ups, he was the one getting attention from a sweet child. My father
was even more elated when Tutul started staring into his face,
gently stroking his cheeks with his tiny hands.

During an awkward silence in the conversation, suddenly
Tutul's voice rang out: 'Mrinal-kaku, why is your face like that of a
monkey?'

My father continued to make films, but popular success eluded him. After his fourth or fifth film was released, the atmosphere at home was, as usual, tense. My father restlessly waited to hear what people thought about it. Whenever anyone visited, the first thing he'd ask was whether they had seen his film and, if so, what they thought of it.

One morning, an old acquaintance dropped in. He was not necessarily the kind of person who would enjoy my father's films. However, my father could not afford to be picky with his reviewers any more, and after a few pleasantries, he asked, 'Did you see my film?' The man nodded and looked up, in deep concentration, as if waiting for the right words, and then finally said, 'Aamar kintu oto kharap lageni'—I didn't think it was too bad. The man had assumed that, by then, my father must have accepted that the film was a complete failure. Out of extreme kindness, he wanted to make my father feel a little better.

When I was in Class Four or Five, on a late evening in early February, on the eve of Saraswati Puja, my friends and I decided to erect a puja pandal. This was when we lived at Manoharpukur Road. Since the road ended at the slum, we could erect the pandal right in the middle of the street, just a couple of houses down from our flat. This was the first puja organized entirely by my friends, the younger group of children on our street. It was a lot of hard work—going door to door to raise funds, running after pedestrians who passed through our area with a booklet of coupons, each valued at 5 paisa. It takes a lot of 5-paisa coupons to add up to a meaningful sum of money. All that hard work paid off when we finally saw our little bamboo pandal housing our proportionately small idol of Saraswati.

Since our street ended in a slum, my friend circle included more children who lived in those tin-roofed houses than those who lived in the brick buildings on the main street. I was always envious of the extra freedom enjoyed by my friends from the slum. They could stay out longer, study a lot less, always go barefoot and do quite a few other things that I'd rather not mention. Therefore, they had no problem spending the night in the puja pandal itself. I, on the other hand, knew it wouldn't be an easy sell in my family.

My father, whom I didn't take very seriously, was out that evening, so I brought it up with my mother. As expected, the immediate answer was an emphatic 'No'. However, after hours of pleading and rational justification, she finally agreed. The deal was that I could not step out of the pandal, so that she could always see me from her window. I also had to promise that if I felt sleepy, I would come back home to bed and not spend the night in the pandal. Having won that tough battle, relieved, and finally feeling free, I proudly went off to my friends.

It was around 10.30 at night when my father came home and heard about my plans. Suddenly, I spotted him coming towards the pandal. As he walked beneath the dim street lamp, his long shadow slowly circled him like the hands of a clock. There was something fateful about it. I immediately sensed trouble and got ready for a confrontation. My friends also noticed the tension on my face, and slowly moved away. As he drew closer, I was relieved to notice that he looked completely relaxed. He walked into the pandal, and started looking at the decorations, ignoring me. When he started asking my friends questions about the decor, I finally relaxed. Clearly, he'd talked with my mother and accepted the situation. Nevertheless, it felt a little weird to see him taking so much interest in our activities—it was so unlike him.

After my friends answered all his questions, he finally noticed my presence in one corner of the pandal. He walked towards me and wrapped an arm around my shoulder. With an ambiguous smile on his face, he pulled me close, lowered his lips to my ear and whispered, 'Come back home—or I'll start dancing here.'

The vision of my father dancing on the street in front of all my friends was horrifying and incredible, but not necessarily improbable. I had been convinced for a long time already that my father was significantly eccentric, so I could not put it past him to execute his absurd plan. Without creating a scene, I slowly untangled myself from his embrace, casually walked back home, closed the door behind me and then burst into tears—partly at my defeat, but also at the thought of my lifelong predicament of sacrificing my pleasures in order to better hide his eccentricities from the prying eyes of the world.

In early 2000, my mother was in a hospital for surgery. My father would visit her during the afternoon visiting hours. One day, as he was getting out of his car, he noticed a crowd of reporters with cameras and recording gear milling around in front of the hospital lobby. He was curious at first, then realized it must be because some celebrity was in the same hospital. As he walked towards the lift, a few reporters spotted him and came rushing to ask if he had come to see 'Mamata-di'. The Opposition leader, Mamata Banerjee, apparently injured during a demonstration the day before, had been admitted to that very hospital for a check-up. He replied in the negative; he was there to see Gita, his wife. Then he went upstairs and spent the afternoon with my mother, and came back home when the visiting period was over.

Next morning, while going through his usual stack of Bengali and English newspapers, a small story caught his eye in a local Bengali daily: it was about my mother's hospitalization, and obviously the result of his brief interaction with the reporters the previous afternoon. Not too many people knew about my mother's illness, and the reporter must have run out of more interesting stories. Later that morning, as more people saw the story, the phone calls began. 'How is Gita-di?' 'What's happened to Boudi?' 'When is Mashima coming home?' Like most people, my father was not too eager to answer them all. As the number of calls increased and the number of questions multiplied, he got a bit impatient. After a few more calls, he changed his answer. Whenever someone asked about what happened to my mother, he said, 'Gita is having a baby.' Considering her age, his response would be met with a stunned silence at the other end. Then the caller would thank him and hang up, probably to more fully grapple with his answer.

In our family, we all learnt the hard way to never disclose any sensitive information to my father because he was certain to divulge it at an awkward moment simply to embarrass us. I remember, right after we got married, Nisha came back from her research lab one day and shared a rumour she had heard about matchmaking attempts for Ray's son, Sandip. Nisha warned Bondhu to not pass it on, as it was most likely a falsehood. My father said, 'Of course,' and went back to whatever he was doing. A little later, sitting around our dining table, we could see him calling someone on the phone. When the caller picked up, my father said, 'Manik-babu, Nisha was telling me that Babu is getting married?' He said this looking straight at Nisha and with a smirk on his face. We don't know how Ray reacted to the question, but Nisha quickly learnt to not trust Bondhu on such matters ever again.

Another anecdote. From 1983–84, when two of the biggest names in Indian cinema, Shabana Azmi and Smita Patil, were together for a film festival or a shoot. Smita had worked in my father's *Akaler Shandhaney*, and Shabana had just finished working in *Khandhar*. My father was fond of both, and they of him. Each of them wanted to work with him again. It may be safe to say that there was some degree of professional rivalry between the two, as they often competed for similar roles and directors. My father was already looking for actors for his next film, and both Shabana and Smita had made it clear that they would love to be considered.

One day, he wrote two identical notes, one to Shabana and another to Smita, saying he would like to discuss his next film as soon as possible. He put the notes in two different envelopes but intentionally put Shabana's name on the one carrying Smita's note and Smita's name on the one carrying Shabana's, and then sent them through a friend who was going to where the two actors were staying. The courier slipped the notes under each actor's door.

Each one must have opened her envelope expectantly, only to discover that the note was intended for the other.

The next morning, each dutifully handed over their note to the other, explaining how Mrinal-da's mail had got muddle up. But when the notes were read, they immediately realized what was going on. Hopefully, it eased the silent tension between them, and they managed to have a good laugh over it.

A few years later, in December 1986, I was visiting my parents when the news arrived that Smita had died, only thirty-one. My father went into a shocked silence. We were all watching television in our dining room when Shabana came on, and gave one of the most touching eulogies—full of professional respect and dignified restraint. My father never got the chance to work with Smita again, but he did work with Shabana in two of his later films.

Towards the end of his life, he became quite grave. Fewer friends visited him; most of them were dead or too old to visit. Nisha and I were away, except for our visits every few months. His body was slowly breaking down. Most of the time, he sat alone, reading his books and newspapers or writing. There were a few moments, though, when the right set of people would gather, and we could once again hear the same levity in his voice.

OUR ENCOUNTERS WITH RELIGION

I spent my early years, from two to fifteen, in our Manoharpukur Road flat. We occupied a portion of the ground floor while the rest of the house belonged to our landlords, a family of eight. The parents and their five children and one of their uncles, plus a small number of floating relatives. They were a deeply religious family—religion was the central theme not only of their spiritual life but also their cultural life. Three of the children were dedicated singers, but their music was primarily devotional. So deep was their religiosity that they defied one of the most vital tenets of Bengali-hood—our love for fish and meat—and were strict vegetarians. Such was the household where I grew up.

My mother had a confused sense of religiosity. On the one hand, she grew up in a time and place where one was religious because there was no other way to be. Her mother, for example, spent all her free time in front of her little shrine. Yet, in my mother's youth, she came in contact with a group of communist activists who were all declared atheists, and then she ended up marrying one. Pinched between these two extremes, she chose to stay in the middle. When asked, she would say she was not a believer. But not wanting to risk annoying the all-powerful in practice, she had a couple of idols and a picture of Ramakrishna tucked away in our closet. She would offer her prayers without much fanfare. On special occasions, she would put some flowers before them.

On some evenings, she would take me to a neighbourhood Kali temple, and I would see her close her eyes and pray with deep sincerity. These visits were especially thrilling to me ever since I learnt that this particular Kali temple used to belong to a band of notorious dacoits, who would pray there before going off on one of their missions. The darkness of that little secluded temple, the silence, the whiff of the incense, the occasional ring of the bell, and above all, my mother's sense of desperation as she prayed with closed eyes, whatever she prayed for, drew me in. I wanted it all to be true. I wanted her prayers to be answered.

The neighbourhood was also ritualistically religious. It was hard for me to tell the level of belief, but everyone practised it unquestioningly. Growing up in that environment, there was no option but to accept all of it as part of one's life. Therefore, I found it odd and a little embarrassing that my father didn't seem to care about religion. I had never seen him make the customarily respectful gestures in front of an idol. He would brush his mother aside if she ever tried to touch his forehead with flowers from her altar. He never made a big show out of it, but he avoided participating in these rituals. I was too young to understand what it meant, and attributed this behaviour as part of all the other eccentricities he seemed to possess.

When I was six, my father was shooting his third film, *Baishey Shravana* (1960). There was a sequence where he wanted to show the passage of time, and he decided to depict a year by showing a quick succession of various goddesses representing the various seasons. His team commissioned the idol-makers to make miniature versions of the idols. After the shoot, one of those idols ended up in our bedroom. One morning, my mother noticed, to her shock and surprise, that I was performing the usual puja rituals before it, but that, instead of flowers, I was using bits of the reed broom used to clean our room. Utterly blasphemous, to use the most impious objects for the gods! Before I could further disrespect the goddess, the idol was quickly removed from our household.

A year later, I was at the market with Anu and saw a cluster of Saraswati idols being sold in preparation for the upcoming Saraswati Puja. I begged my uncle to purchase one, and he eventually succumbed. When we walked in with the idol, my mother quickly proclaimed that it was not a toy for me to play with but must be treated with the respect, and a proper ritual must be performed.

Anu was always good with craftwork, and immediately took up the challenge of creating a decorative background for the idol. He found a piece of old cloth, dyed it with clay and mud and draped it over our living-room furniture to create the appearance of a mountain range. The Saraswati idol was placed in front. We had a small fish tank; a hole was cut in the cloth, so the fish tank was visible through it. It all looked fantastic!

The next day was the auspicious day, so my mother tried to arrange for a Brahmin priest to come home and perform the rituals. However, it was too late to get one; they were already booked.

My father's friend Nripen Ganguly was visiting that morning. To salvage the situation, my mother asked him if he could perform the ritual. Nripen-kaka was a Brahmin and had some familiarity with the practices from his younger days. He reluctantly agreed. This was perhaps a rare moment when a communist and an atheist actively performed a Hindu ritual. My father was greatly bemused by this scene and, at one point, held his burning cigarette to the lips of the goddess so it would appear she was smoking. This was the first time I saw him cross that line; it made my mother very angry, and I burst into tears.

Many years later, as I looked back on those days, I was grateful that my father had not once tried to indoctrinate me into his beliefs. He never tried to dissuade me from my childish religiosity. Apart from that one moment with the cigarette, he never questioned my actions. He just stayed aloof and let things take their course. Anyone familiar with most left-liberal households from that era would know how rare this was. Most of the other children I knew who grew up in similar families were bombarded with ideas long before they were ready to process them. I was spared such an intellectual onslaught and allowed complete freedom to form my own mind.

A few years after the incident with my Saraswati idol, I was talking to my small group of friends. Somehow the topic of Creation came up. I had a Muslim Sindhi friend, and he shared what he knew to be the Creation story. Someone else told the story of Samudra Manthan from Hindu mythology. A Christian among us told the story of Adam and Eve. They were all engaging tales, and like any child, I wanted to believe my friends. Yet, that is when doubt first entered my mind: How can all of them be correct? I still remember that was the first moment that I thought: perhaps they are all stories, and no more. It took many more years for this seed of doubt to grow in me. Finally, as I became smitten with my love for science, my own atheism started to take form.

Many decades later, in 2006, I read a great book by evolutionary biologist Richard Dawkins called *The God Delusion*. I gave a copy of the book to my father and wrote inside,

To Bondhu,
who allowed me to think freely
so that I can be a better atheist
Babu
April 15, 2007

When I was twelve, I used to go to a school run by a group of left-leaning cultural elites. It was a great experience and gave me early exposure to the world of art and culture. One day, we were asked to write an essay on our favourite writer. I picked a popular adventure and detective-story writer called Hemendra Kumar Roy. I later heard that my choice caused somewhat of a stir among the teachers because the expected answer, especially from the son of Mrinal Sen, would have been someone holding a higher position in the cultural hierarchy—and not a mere detective-story writer. Looking back, I must once again thank my father for giving me that space. He respected my mind as much as he respected his own. Many parents do not want to take that chance, and try to ensure their children learn to think the 'right way'. If we had children, perhaps I would have also made that mistake. But my father decided to take that chance, and patiently waited for my mind to evolve on its own.

During my college days, I remember having a serious conversation with him during which I said that science was also a belief system at some level. Some things were beyond proof, even within the scientific method. For example, we must believe in reason to believe in science. My argument was not flawless, and I probably would have argued differently if I had the conversation today, but after hearing me out, my father commented that I may start believing in God one day. That was the only time I realized his concern about my position on religion, but he did not push it any further. He was concerned, but he still did not want to impose.

Despite his strong ideology, my father could somehow manage to remain open-minded. All his life, I have seen him embracing people with beliefs and lifestyles very different from his own. Once he discovered something interesting in them, he could easily overlook other differences. In my life, I have tried hard to follow that but mostly failed. I could never muster the intellectual generosity and humility that one needs to practise it.

I remember my first adventure with my father when we took the tram to get lost in the dense morning fog. He assured me he was there but did not hold my hand to show me the way. As then, throughout his life, he allowed me to find my own way, which is the greatest gift a parent can offer. People often ask me why I did not make films. I guess that is why.

THE REVOLUTIONARY YEARS

The local politics in our state of West Bengal started to take a turn in 1967. I was in my early teens, and the promise of a change excited me. For the first time since Independence in 1947, a left-wing party was in control of our state government. A united front led by one of the two Marxist factions of the Communist Party of India defeated the party that had always ruled the state and was still in power at the national level. However, just a few months later, the Centre first dismissed the state government, then handed over control to a minority party aligned with the Centre's politics. Eventually, the state was brought directly under central rule. The following two years were marked by violent protests throughout the city. For the first time, I felt a connection with my father on political issues. There were frequent general strikes—we would intently listen to the news on the radio for reports of violence, and then venture out to inspect the situation. He also started shooting these events with no particular goal, and later used that footage in various films.

In 1969, another election was held, and the Left Front came back to power. During the same period, another political movement was taking shape. The Maoist faction of the Communist Party organized a peasant uprising in the Naxalbari region of northern West Bengal. This group was gaining in strength, and on

1 May 1969, called their first public rally in Calcutta. It was a very tense day, for the Marxist faction had also called a meeting on adjacent grounds. I went to see the Maoist rally and heard the call they made to students to organize and join the revolution. While I was listening to the Maoist speeches, I could also see the Marxist crowd nearby.

I came home excited. My father wanted to know all about it, so I told him about both meetings. Later that night, I saw him pick up a copy of *Liberation*, the English-language publication of the Maoist party that I had brought back from the rally. An article from the Maoist leader called for all students to give up school, leave home and work in the villages in order to organize the peasants and start the revolution.

The following day, we both woke up early. My father looked disturbed. He came over and sat next to me and said, 'I read the article. Are you planning to go? If you go, I will come with you.'

I had no such plans, as I wasn't sure I agreed with their agenda. More importantly, I did not have the courage or the conviction to take up the life of a revolutionary. I had first-hand contact with many such people, and their stories of police torture were all too real to me. I was not sure that I could endure the suffering. So, no matter how romantic it sounded to a fifteen-year-old, I had absolutely no plans to leave home.

However, my father did not know that and thought I well might. Like any father, he did not want me to, but perhaps he did not want to stand in my way either. So the next best thing he could do was attach his safety and well-being to my revolutionary aspirations, and hope that might prevent me from going.

Over the next two years, the violence around the city escalated. Every day there were clashes with the police and conflicts between the two factions of the Communist Party. Innumerable young people lost their lives. There were senseless killings everywhere. One day, a traffic policeman was stabbed and murdered right on our doorstep. It was the policy of the ultra-left to kill policemen and create an atmosphere of terror. My father was deeply distressed by that, and continued to be afraid for my safety. After any such incident, the typical police reaction would be to pick up all the young people in that neighbourhood for interrogation.

He was deeply conflicted by all this and could not bring himself to support the senseless violence. Nor could he support the outright rejection of every old cultural and political figure in the name of cultural revolution. Nor could he tolerate the mortal split between the two factions of the left. Yet, he was empathetic with the young students dying in the name of revolution.

He was editing his film in New Theatres Studio, Tollygunge. Most people had stopped working there, since it was a hotbed of Naxalite Maoist activities. There were frequent police raids on the studio grounds as the students often used it as a hideout. One day, he told some of the students that if there was a raid, a few of them could come into his editing room and pretend to be a part of his team. They should just make sure that the number was small enough to be credible.

A few days later, there was a police raid. Though no one came to his editing room, he saw a young person climb up a nearby tree and hide in the upper branches. By the time the police arrived, my father was relieved to see that the person was safely hidden behind the dense foliage. But only a few minutes later, the young man threw a handmade bomb at the police. They immediately spotted him and shot him down. His revolutionary anger overcame his sense of safety, and that was his fatal mistake.

It was impossible for my father not to react to what was happening around him, and so his films became increasingly political. In 1973, he made *Padatik*, which reflected the political confusion he faced during this period. He questioned the politics of the far left but as an insider. He often used to say that the line between criticism and slander is a thin one. Many on the extreme left viewed it as a betrayal, but I think he reacted with compassion and political foresight.

The Maoist movement was eventually destroyed by the relentless assault of the police and by the disillusionment inside the party. In 1977, the moderate left party, the Marxist faction, returned to power and remained in power for the next thirty-four years. My father was again frustrated by the left's complacency and its inability to make much meaningful change. Still, he was heartbroken when a populist party finally pushed the left coalition out. He carried that bitterness till the end, when the left had become marginalized.

His connection with Marxist ideology was profound, and it essentially defined his moral being from his earliest years. He discovered it as a teenager when he landed in Calcutta, alone in a big city. It provided an ethical framework for his existence and survival, connected him to his friends and offered him the security of his being part of something bigger. For a boy growing up in one corner of the world, it was his way of feeling connected to fellow travellers in the strange and faraway worlds of Europe, the Americas and other parts of Asia. Above all, as he witnessed and experienced all sorts of injustice in the world around him, this was the ideology that offered him a way out. It allowed him to dream of a more just and fairer society.

He grew up admiring the few scattered successes of this ideology, and created a mental image of these utopian societies. The first time he had the opportunity to visit one of them was in 1965, when he was selected as part of a peace delegation to the Soviet Union and Finland. It was a three-stop trip to Tashkent, Moscow and Helsinki. By then, the Communist Party of India had already undergone a split between the pro-Soviet faction and those that were further to the left.

My father came back deeply disillusioned. Instead of finding the transformed land that was promised in all the books and films he had admired, he found a place overwhelmed with bureaucracy and where everyone feared the all-pervasive state-security apparatus. He saw an acute shortage of essential things instead of the promised abundance. He saw the greed for Western artefacts in the eyes of the general population. He saw how staff in restaurants were eager to pamper the Western clients but ignored people from Asia and Africa. It was a rude awakening.

Once he came back home, he mentioned his views to his friends, and they reached the ears of many of his Communist Party friends too who were not happy to see a Marxist openly criticizing the Soviet land. One of the founders of my school, Patha Bhavan—Uma Sehanabis, and her husband, Chinmohan—were a highly respected couple among the city's cultural elite. They had been the first to invite my parents over for a postnuptial dinner. Uma-di was furious that my father criticized the Soviet system, and they had a big argument. I was eleven, and a huge admirer of Uma-di. It was difficult for me to witness my favourite teacher disagreeing with my father.

Many years later, in 1977, my parents visited China for the first and only time. This time he came back impressed. He wanted to see a place and its people transformed by a cultural revolution, which he did. He did not question the strictly controlled exposure offered by the state apparatus and accepted what he saw as the broad reality. I remember him saying he'd seen a new breed of humans, leading a modest but morally astute life. He had not seen the greed in their eyes as he had in Russia.

Part of his itinerary included a visit to an elementary-school classroom. He saw posters stating that the student who arrived at the school first would have the privilege of sweeping the floors. He asked the teacher if students did come early, and was told there was serious competition among students to be the first, for the bragging rights. He immediately compared it to a local Bengali saying which essentially discourages students from going to school too early. Many of us have heard the statement, 'Why are you in such a rush—are you going to sweep the floors?' My father saw a new ethics in the Chinese people that were the polar opposite of what we had been taught.

Children as young as six or seven were taught 'politics' in that same school. He was curious, and asked the teacher what the lessons comprised. The teacher showed him a typical politics lesson. It consisted of a series of unlabelled pictures. The first was of an older woman carrying a basket full of fruit. The second was of the woman now fallen on the ground, the fruit scattered all around her. The third was of the woman staring at her empty basket. At this point, the students were asked what they would do if they were present at the scene. Of course, there were many answers, but the teacher tried to encourage those which involved the children helping the woman put her fruit back in her basket. My father was deeply impressed to see that politics, at its fundamental level, was not about statecraft but simple, moral acts.

The only negative experience he had while visiting China was to realize the complete isolation of the Chinese filmmakers. None of the filmmakers he met had any exposure to world cinema. Not only had they never heard of Western filmmakers, they had never heard of Asian filmmakers like Akira Kurosawa either. This was surprising to him, but he still failed to connect it with the isolation and state control that existed in China.

In Beijing, they were taken to Mao's mausoleum. He and my mother stood in a long line for their turn to enter. The atmosphere was sombre. As my mother finally reached the embalmed body of Mao, she burst into sobs. My father asked her what had happened. She said that she was reminded of the many young students in

Bengal who had given up their lives out of faith in this one man. This event must have stayed with my father; many years later, while making *Mahaprithibi* (1991), that is what formed the psychological and moral basis of the mother's character. As Marxist edifices crumbled everywhere, as the world seemed to agree that it had all been a big mistake, the mother asked the simple question: Had her son's death and sacrifice been rendered meaningless?

This was a question that became increasingly important to my father as he aged. I had many conversations with him regarding all the new facts surfacing about communist states. I shared with him the innumerable excesses performed by Stalin in the name of revolution. I shared the first-hand experiences of those who had been imprisoned in the labour camps of Siberia. Later, I shared many books of first-person narratives from the Cultural Revolution during Mao's reign. I asked why there had not been a leadership change in Cuba in all these years. He listened to me with deep attention. I could see the gathering pain in his face as he heard these reassessments. What was just a re-evaluation of history to me was to him the dismantling of the plinth of his intellectual self. He was always a questioner of dogmatic beliefs, and never became a member of any communist party for precisely that reason. Jokingly, he would describe himself as a 'private Marxist'. Yet, as external criticisms mounted, as the Soviet system crumbled, as China admitted that the Cultural Revolution was a mistake and as the Chinese state and its people began to chase material affluence, my father began to feel more and more isolated and defeated.

Once, around 1999, he was invited to be the chairman of the jury at a film festival in Sochi, Russia. My mother's health was not good enough for travel, nor was she confident of letting my father travel alone. So Nisha agreed to accompany him. One day, when my father had an afternoon off, they both went to see a dacha used by Stalin. It had been converted into a museum, with a life-sized replica of Stalin sitting at his desk. Suddenly, another visitor, perhaps an American, put her lit cigarette to Stalin's lips in jest. This infuriated my father, and he scolded the tourist for showing such disrespect to history and tried to remind her of Stalin's positive role during the Second World War. I am sure she found it strange; from where she came, Stalin's image was not significantly different from that of Hitler. The story reminded me of the time, many decades ago, when my father held a lit cigarette to the lips of a clay Saraswati idol, a gesture that had enraged my mother. He must have felt he had permission to do so because he had no respect for the idol, and that it was fair for him to express that feeling through humour. However, it was impossible for him to imagine that someone may have a similar indifference or even disrespect for one of his early heroes.

People of his generation were probably better off not knowing about this shift in history. None of us know how history will view our era, say, fifty years from now. Will the current views prevail, or are we going to take a different perspective? History is never entirely objective, and the politics of the present influence all historical interpretations. My father lived a little too long to enter a historical phase where most of the world decided to move away from what he believed to be the truth. He lived a very lonely life during his final years. Physical loneliness is painful, but intellectual loneliness can be so much worse.

A lighter moment during the making of *Antareen*.
PHOTO Subhash Nandy.

ABOVE. Ma and her family, Uttarpara.
PHOTO Nisha Ruparel-Sen.

BELOW. Ma during our wedding ceremony.
PHOTO Unknown.

ABOVE. Leaving for Chicago.
PHOTO Unknown.

BELOW. Anu with Nisha, the day she was to leave for Chicago to join me.
PHOTO Unknown.

ABOVE. In Chicago, 1989. PHOTO Nisha Ruparel-Sen.
CENTRE, AND BELOW. Our family in Chicago. PHOTOS Jagriti Ruparel.

ABOVE LEFT. Anu (Anup Kumar) at our Motilal Nehru flat. PHOTO Kunal Sen.
ABOVE RIGHT. Anu and I in Santiniketan. PHOTO Mrinal Sen.
BELOW. Ma, Anu and I in Patna. PHOTO Unknown.

RIGHT. Ma and I on my birthday.
PHOTO Unknown.

BELOW. Ma and I in Santiniketan.
PHOTO Mrinal Sen.

ABOVE. With Ma and Bondhu, during the shooting of *Mrigayaa*.
PHOTO Subhash Nandy.

BELOW. Mamata Shankar in our Motilal Nehru Road flat.
PHOTO Kunal Sen.

ABOVE. During the shooting of *Khandhar*.
PHOTO Subhash Nandy.

BELOW. Nisha and I with Shabana, during the shooting of *Khandhar*.
PHOTO Subhash Nandy.

Lunch at Cannes, 2010. PHOTO Nisha Ruparel-Sen.

ABOVE. Bondu and Ray. PHOTO Unknown.
BELOW. A birthday evening with Buddhadev Bhattacharya. PHOTO Kunal Sen.

With friends on his last birthday. PHOTO Unknown.

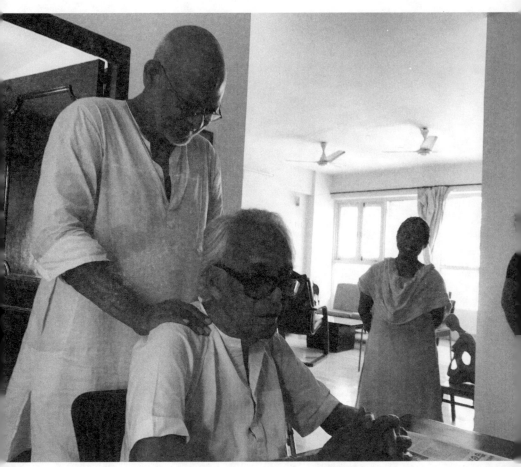

Massaging Bondhu's shoulders. PHOTO Nisha Ruparel-Sen.

ABOVE, LEFT. The Brussels winter forced them to wear Western clothes. PHOTO Kunal Sen.

ABOVE, RIGHT. Ma and I, Brussels, 1985. PHOTO Nisha Ruparel-Sen.

BELOW. Breakfast time. PHOTO Kunal Sen.

ABOVE. Jesting with Stalin.
PHOTO Nisha Ruparel-Sen.

BELOW. Kunal, Mrinal,
Marx, Engels. Berlin.
PHOTO Nisha Ruparel-Sen.

ABOVE. Lunch at Frankfurt, 2010.
PHOTO Unknown.

LEFT. When he needed a helping
hand. Frankfurt, 2010.

PHOTO Nisha Ruparel-Sen.

Birthday dinner at Cannes, 2010. PHOTO Nisha Ruparel-Sen.

PART 2

Filmmaker

PREPARATIONS

It is well known that my father deviated from his written screen-plays more often than not. However, he did not start out that way.

He learnt how to make films through trial and error, which is certainly not the best way to learn anything. In the early days, he tried to follow the conventional steps of writing a tight script and following that during the production process. But the atmosphere in our home was not conducive to any concentrated work. A steady stream of friends occupied our tiny living room, which was also a bedroom for my uncle Anu, my place to study and the only pas-sageway connecting the kitchen and our bedroom to the outside world. It was clear to my father that he could not focus and write a script there. He may also have been influenced by the romantic notion of writers situating themselves in an isolated location, per-haps amid the vastness of nature, in order to do their creative work.

One such place he found was in the little-known beachfront town of Digha. It was not the busy tourist destination it is today, but a tiny cluster of holiday homes and low-cost hotels along the sea. The main attraction was its proximity to Calcutta, and hotel rates well within the levels he could justify.

Digha did not have a round-the-clock electricity supply in those days. Power was turned on during the early evening hours

73

and then shut off around eight or nine. The steady sea breeze from the Bay of Bengal, blowing over the pristine and uncrowded sands, meant that fans were not really required in the homes and hotels.

On his second visit to one such hotel, perhaps during the making of either *Punascha* (1961) or *Abasheshe* (1963), he was in a ground-floor room. Apart from the bed, there was a small table and chair facing the open window. The electricity was already turned off, so he was writing by candlelight. Beyond the small circle of flickering light on his table, there was the darkness and the gentle rumble of the waves. Suddenly, he heard a deep, masculine voice, asking him if he wanted a massage. My father was never a brave man under most circumstances; later he told us he was convinced it was a ghost. Realizing that a simple wooden door was no protection against a spirit that could walk through that material barrier, and because he did not want to annoy it with a refusal, he lifted the wooden bar that lay across the door and opened it.

The voice then instructed him to lie face down on his bed, which he immediately did.

The massage started from his lower back and slowly moved upward. As it reached the area of his neck, he remembered from his childhood stories that the favourite mode of execution for ghosts is to wring the victim's neck. He resigned himself to his fate and waited for that final moment. However, to his surprise, the hands started moving downward again. He reasoned that the ghost must be having fun, playing with its hapless prey. This continued for what felt like an eternity.

Finally, the hands came off, and after a short pause, the voice said, 'Babu, paisa.'

His residual rational mind concluded that if an apparition asked for money, it must have human needs, and thus he was saved. I am not sure how long he stayed there after this experience.

While making his next film, he again said goodbye to us and went off on his script-writing trip. After a couple of days, one of our family friends stopped by. Shantu Mukherjee was probably our only friend in those days who owned a car. He was a close friend of Hemanta Mukherjee, the famous singer who produced my father's *Neel Akasher Neechey* (1958). Shantu-kaka and his wife told my mother that a new Canadian steam engine was parked at Howrah Station, and I might enjoy a close look at it. Like most children, I was fascinated by locomotives, so I got ready in minutes, and we all bundled into their car.

Once we reached the station, Shantu-kaka parked his car, got out and began to walk. The rest of us followed. My heart was pounding with the excitement of seeing the technological marvel. But, instead of walking towards the platforms, Shantu-kaka started climbing the stairs. He explained that one could have a better view of the train from upstairs. We walked down a corridor and stopped in front of a door. Shantu-kaka knocked, and after a short delay, the door opened—and standing there was my father!

My father had come to the station to catch the train to his seafront hideout, but then saw that rooms were available for rent in the guestroom wing. That morning, Shantu-kaka happened to be at the station for some reason, and spotted my father on the balcony of a guest room. We are not sure whether the ghost incident had anything to do with it, but for some reason he decided not to travel any further and wrote the screenplay in a room overlooking one of the busiest, smokiest and noisiest stations in the world. I never quite understood why he would pick such a place to write anything, but he did.

As the years progressed, his range of script-writing locations kept shrinking. The last time he wrote a script outside our living room was in 1968 for *Bhuvan Shome*. We still lived in our ground-floor flat on Manoharpukur Road. He had agreed to do the film after his friend Arun Kaul essentially locked him up in a small office in Bombay for a few hours to write a synopsis for a film proposal that would be presented to the state-funded Film Finance Corporation (FFC) for a grant. Surprisingly, the FFC agreed to the unusual proposal he'd created, and now he had to expand the short story into a full-length film.

This time he chose a hotel about a ten-minute walk from our flat. Hotel Raj was probably the only hotel in the area, intended for middle-class visitors from southern India. My father always had a maniacal eagerness to receive his mail and phone messages. I was fourteen then, and my task was to carry all the mail from that day, plus all the phone messages, to him every afternoon. In return, I got to eat a dosa delivered to his room from the restaurant below. I think he took about five days to write that script, but that was the film in which he started to improvise during the shoot. The location in the Saurashtra region of Gujarat triggered ideas that were impossible to imagine in a dingy hotel room on Manohar-pukur Road. Working with actors like Utpal Dutt, Sadhu Meher and Shekhar Chatterjee, as well as the charming Suhasini Mulay, plus a fresh new crew from the Film and Television Institute of India (FTII) in Pune making their first film, created an atmosphere of creativity that a written script could not restrain.

I am not sure if one can read something more fundamental about his creative process from his later choice of crowded and busy places to write his scripts. His initial choice of desolate locations was perhaps driven by romantic notions of writers needing isolation and solitude. But I don't think that was the real him. He genuinely loved the chaos and cacophony of the city, and I believe he drew inspiration from it, be it from the hustle and bustle of a train station or a congested street. Whenever he used panoramic shots of the city, showing the endless rooftops, I remember he always looked for a spot where there were not too many trees.

The best example of a location inspiring a film sequence was in the bhoot-bangla or haunted-house sequence in *Bhuvan Shome*. The team was driving to their location, which was an area where a vast number of migratory birds congregate, when my father noticed a small two-storey building. They stopped to investigate, and were told it was an observation post created by some member of the local royalty. My father was fascinated by the house and decided to shoot there itself. He took a little time to jot down the sequence and dialogue. What emerged was perhaps one of the most memorable sequences of the film, where a young girl relates the fairy-tale-like description of old times when kings and queens visited this place to relax, swing on the jhoola and watch the birds. In the process, the peasant girl herself transforms into a princess.

Of course, there are limitations and perils of on-the-spot scripting—it is easy to miss things. In the final version of the film, there is a shot of the girl telling her tale while the camera stays on her feet peeping out of her beautiful embroidered ghagra. This shot was not captured during the original shoot, but my father felt it was needed while he was editing the film in Bombay. The ghagra was still available, and so was the cameraman and his assistant, but Suhasini was not. So the assistant cameraman, H. K. Verma, who was a man of a more petite build, was made to wear the ghagra while K. K. Mahajan took the shot. It all worked out in the end.

In 1969, we moved to the slightly larger and airy apartment near Deshapriya Park. It still had just one bedroom and one living room, but it was not as congested as our previous place. Between that and my father's increased confidence that he could manage without a fully structured script, he never again left home to write his screenplays.

He also discovered another benefit of writing at home: getting continuous feedback from a few people like my mother and me. Every evening he would read out his day's output to both of us. I was growing up with some degree of opinion. My father listened to what I had to say with intense attention, whether I was ready for that attention or not. I don't think I had a developed a sense of anything yet, but I believe my father trusted me to be brutally honest, which I was. Perhaps a little too much so. Like any adolescent young man, I felt I had the responsibility to rebel, and like the feedback I would give him after seeing the film, I was more eager to find faults in my father's thinking and his scripts rather than praise him for his successes. He must have found that helpful. As I said before, it is hard for successful people in India to hear contrarian views as they tend to surround themselves with sycophants. Much later, talking to Satyajit Ray one day, he'd asked Ray if he felt lonely, and Ray had replied, 'Terribly so.'

However, the principal value of these sessions was what he got from my mother. He always respected the tough life my mother had experienced and the life lessons and perspectives she had gleaned from it. She was also much more familiar with the dailyness of lower-middle-class life. Since most of his films were set in such an atmosphere, my mother could add details and correct mistakes and help his films look more natural. Even more important was her contribution from an actor's point of view. While listening to the dialogue he'd written, she could point out sections that sounded stiff or would be challenging to say. My father took her advice with all seriousness and was grateful for it.

He always depended on similar feedback from his actors, especially the stronger ones who were more confident in their abilities. He would encourage them to change the dialogue as they saw fit. However, he did not always work with strong actors, and such meaningful feedback was not always available. My mother also didn't accompany him during most of his shoots. Looking back, I can see many situations where his dialogue could have been more casual and authentic if such feedback had indeed been available.

I remember a sequence from *Chalchitra* (1981). The mother, played by my mother, was bargaining with a woman who bartered stainless-steel utensils for old clothes. The character was played by a real-life vendor who did exactly that for a living. My mother suggested they not follow the script at all, but do it extempore. The result was an entirely believable and wonderfully alive sequence. I don't believe it would have looked as natural if they had tried to use scripted dialogue or attempted to train the woman to learn and then repeat her lines.

But in *Kharij* (1982), there was one sequence where this extempore approach largely failed. The actors were asked to play with the on-screen family's child to keep him distracted. They ended up using a pair of slippers as a toy, and talking simultaneously. But no adult would encourage a child to handle a couple of dirty slippers in real life, and their chatter too sounds less than natural. In this case, the actors could not use their freedom effectively, and my father failed to pick up on it during the shoot.

His confidence that he could improvise once failed him entirely. In 1970, he agreed to work on another film produced by his friend Arun Kaul. It was a Hindi-language film to be shot in a village near Patna, Bihar. He was working on the story of *Ek Adhuri Kahani* (1971), had selected the actors and was to leave for his location in a few days, but I believe he began to doubt the project and could not put down anything on paper.

The crew had already arrived at their location and was starting to prepare. Kaul was on a very tight budget as he'd borrowed money from the government. The night before he was supposed to leave for Patna, my father told us that he would be so relieved if he died that night—and we knew he meant it. However, he survived and left the following day. His crew members told us later that after each day's shoot, he would stay up until late into the night, trying to write for the next day, sleep for a few hours, then get up early in the morning for another day of work. The result was an uneven film, clearly showing his heart was not in it. It is impossible to say whether things would have been different if he was improvising his way through a film that he believed in. Was the failure due to a lack of preparation or conviction? Despite the film being a failure in his eyes, it won the Special Jury Award at the Mannheim Film Festival.

I would have loved to watch one of my father's films and then compare it with the written screenplay to see how far it deviated, and then wonder, 'Why did *that* happen?' It would have been a great way to understand his creative process. But there is no way to do that, as none of his original screenplays are available any more. There are printed screenplays, but these were created after the fact by watching and transcribing the finished films.

On the other hand, all of Ray's original screenplays and notes are still available and offer a great insight into his creative process. I was fortunate to have worked on a project to create a digital version of the materials for *Goopy Gyne Bagha Byne*. I was mesmerized by the meticulous detail with which he conceived everything. Looking at his script and visual notes, one can see that he imagined almost every shot before it was captured on camera and every detail of the set design. The act of shooting was to materialize a vision he could already see in his mind's eye. Therefore, knowing Ray's style, after seeing one of his films, it is not all that difficult to imagine what the screenplay may look like. You could expect something reasonably close to the film.

That is one type of creative process. But I feel it would have been even more interesting to see my father's scripts, as it is impossible to predict what to expect. There may have been sections faithfully captured on celluloid, but there may have been others that were entirely different.

My father never indulged in nostalgia. He explicitly declared war on nostalgia, as he believed it could distort objectivity and romanticize the past. It is hard to say how much of that was heart-felt and how much an intellectual decision. He used to talk fondly about his childhood days in Faridpur, and there was a hint of nostalgia there. But I must admit I never heard him glorify those memories. He narrated them merely as funny anecdotes, and not with a sense of great loss. Unlike Ritwik-kaka, he never regretted leaving his ancestral home in East Bengal and coming to Calcutta, nor did he display strong emotions about the Partition.

When it came to his films, he had an intense love for his latest production and would furiously defend it. However, with time, that love would fade. A few films maintained their grip on him, but he became increasingly indifferent towards the rest. He often used to say that he wished each film had been a dress rehearsal and that he could make it a second time. Part of that feeling was also because of his improvisational style, where he desired to do things a little differently the next time.

Therefore he never had a deep attachment to his scripts once the films were made. Moreover, he was unbelievably disorganized. Every day he would receive dozens of letters in the post, primarily junk, but he never organized them nor threw away the useless ones. Papers would start piling up on his desk. At some point, my mother would scream that there wasn't an empty spot anywhere, and then he would throw the whole pile away or tie it up with string and shove the bundle under the bed or into some shelf. Each time we moved during my childhood, most of the papers and bundles were discarded.

We can certainly blame my father for the loss of his screenplays and notes, but the question remains: Why didn't we, the people around him, try to save them? I could have tried to archive his film scripts and important correspondence. I do not blame my mother, as she already had her hands full with a million other things. But I could have played a significant role in preserving the physical pieces of my father's work. It is hard to look back and say why I did not. One factor that may have contributed to this was my being raised to believe that I was an independent human being with my own life, aims and aspirations. I was never allowed to think that I was the keeper of my father's legacy. I always believed my future would not depend on his fame. I was convinced I would make my mark in my way, and in my youthful enthusiasm, I even fantasized that I would be famous in my own right. I never looked that far ahead to think that perhaps these papers would be of some value some day, and that I should try to save them for posterity.

Today, I certainly regret that subconscious decision. If there was a way to turn back the clock, I would like to act differently. His production team also did not have the foresight to salvage them. His film assistants and production managers had their copies of the original screenplay, and we have to wonder if any of those copies still exist. It is unlikely that the heat, humidity, dust and lack of space in most of their households have been kind to those papers.

THE ECONOMICS OF AESTHETICS

When my father started making films, his style was largely conventional. He picked slightly unusual subjects, but the process followed the same pattern as the rest of the industry. He preferred using subjects that reflected his sociopolitical views and were modern compared to the times. I don't know anything about his first film, *Raat Bhore*, as he never spoke about it. His second film's hero was a Chinese hawker, and it dealt with his non-romantic relationship with a Bengali housewife and a political worker. My father's third film was about a rural couple with a big age difference, set against the backdrop of the 1943 Bengal Famine that killed about five million people. His subsequent films dealt with divorce and other social situations rarely touched upon by his contemporaries. He also largely avoided melodrama and song sequences, which were the essential ingredients of most Indian films.

Despite their uniqueness in terms of subject matter, these films did follow standard storytelling models. His film crew also mainly consisted of industry people, who brought with them all the conventions of traditional production processes. In his early days, the actors he cast were well tested in the film world, except for a few whom he recruited from his IPTA theatre days. His budgets also mostly followed the usual conventions—neither extravagant nor particularly frugal. I don't have specific numbers, but I guess they cost the same as other family dramas made at the time. Since most of these films were commercial failures, they were unable to recover the investments.

This pattern started to change with *Akash Kusum*, made in 1965. Even though he still used the standard industry production crew and methods, the film's language was noticeably different—it was restless and edgy, and provoked a months-long battle in the press after Ray, almost out of the blue, decided to attack it in a letter to the editor of the *Statesman*. He noticed the stylistic shift, but felt that the film was still conventional, merely wrapped in a modern veneer. It still puzzles me why Ray decided to take up this public battle when his position was so well established; could he have sensed a possible threat from this new style which could one day challenge his own conventional narrative methods?

My father's next film was in the Odia language, which he did not speak. It was the first time he was making a film outside his familiar Bengal. The decision was primarily economic, as locating funding for his films was becoming progressively trickier. Once again, in *Matira Manisha* (1966), one can see a restless shift in his mode of expression. He also used actors who were mostly outsiders to the film industry.

Following *Matira Manisha* came the longest gap in his filmmaking career—because no one was willing to fund him. This gap perhaps pushed him to take stock of his position as a creative artist. He felt the intense urge to use a different language at the same time as he realized it was unlikely to get a large audience. He needed an audience willing to grow with him and learn to appreciate a different aesthetic. But, he realistically concluded, such an audience would always be small and scattered. He also realized that the only way someone would be willing to finance such a film was if the budget could be kept as low as possible. He knew only too well that anyone who spent a lot on a film would try their best to recover their money as well exert more creative control. That is precisely what he did not want; he wanted creative freedom, and the only way he knew to achieve that was to cut production costs. He wanted to challenge the notion that filmmaking was an expensive proposition.

After more than two years, his Bombay-based friend Arun Kaul practically forced him to submit a proposal to the Film Finance Corporation, a governmental agency that was thinking of changing its funding policies. He wrote an outline and asked for a ridiculously small amount to fund a Hindi-language film. If I remember correctly, the budget was one hundred and twenty-five thousand rupees. The choice of Hindi was also driven by the realization that this would give them a much larger audience base than a regional language like Bengali.

This was when my father wanted to discard all the conventions he had followed so far. So he used a film crew composed entirely of first-time technicians. The rest of the team were all outsiders too, including some of the actors. They decided to shoot outdoors, thus cutting down the cost of sets and equipment. He also wanted to keep the shooting time as short as possible, something that strongly impacted the budget. *Bhuvan Shome* was shot in about twenty days, and this was helped by the fact that none of the actors or crew had any conflicting schedules.

After the shooting, he did the editing in Bombay and recorded the music in a small room on quarter-inch tape with Vijay Raghav Rao, a music director who had only worked on documentaries. After finishing all the postproduction work, he returned to Calcutta with a finished film. It was the first film where my mother and I had no inkling about the finished product until the first private screening at the New Theatres Studio.

I still remember that evening. I was fifteen and developing my taste in art, and I was drawn to the newer, more adventurous languages. There was an audience of perhaps a hundred or so. There was dead silence after the film was over, then thunderous applause. Everyone agreed that this film had broken some new barriers, and they were excited to be the first to witness it. I was also overjoyed because the aesthetics of the film exactly matched what I was looking for—a new language and a new energy.

The overall success of *Bhuvan Shome* solidified his conviction that the way to continue to experiment with his medium was by keeping his costs low and reaching those scattered small but sensitive audiences. The film was released in a single theatre in each of the major cities, but with only one screening a day. That allowed praise of the film to spread by word of mouth, and the shows stayed full for much longer. *Bhuvan Shome*'s success was followed by other similar films by directors from all over India, and ushered in what was later named the Indian New Wave.

After *Bhuvan Shome*, which gave him a place in world cinema, locating funding became significantly easier. Not that the financiers expected to make a lot of money, but given their low investment, they felt comfortable that they could get their money back, if not in the domestic market then certainly through foreign sales. There was also the attraction of awards, both from the Indian government and international film festivals. Some of his subsequent financiers primarily looked for the cultural spotlight and cared much less about recovering the cost.

Towards the end of his career, more people wanted to fund him than he was willing to accept. When he stopped making films, there were many offers that said they would use his name and he would only have to oversee the production. They promised to find competent people to do all the running around, which he obviously could not do any more. Of course, he never agreed.

He told me about some of these, and they sounded like they were out of an absurdist play. The financier would suggest a relatively big budget—a bigger budget implies higher production quality and better stars, and the film is easier to market. But my father knew a bigger budget would imply greater moral pressure on him to recover costs and force him to compromise his artistic integrity. Therefore, he would suggest a much smaller budget. Consequently, a negotiation would ensue, except in the wrong direction, where the buyer was willing to pay more and the seller was negotiating for less!

Perhaps he was generalizing too much, but my father often used to say that a look at the home of a filmmaker told him what kind of films he could expect out of that person. He believed that any attempt to please a broad audience necessarily implied creative compromise.

My father and I argued about many things, and one recurring issue was the use of technology in films. Any mention of cutting-edge technologies, like 3D films or computer-generated imagery (CGI), and he would flare up and denounce the film that used it as a cheap, commercial entity, devoid of any artistic merit. I had to agree with most of his specific assertions since most such films are indeed pure Hollywood fantasies, made with the sole purpose of making money. However, I tried to argue that the technologies involved were not to be blamed, as they had the potential to be used creatively to great artistic ends. I had, in those days, very few examples to back up my argument. But I did use Stanley Kubrick's *2001: A Space Odyssey*, one of my favourite films, to show that special effects could be used to create a profound film. That film could not have been made without that technology. He did not challenge the artistic quality of the film, but wasn't ready to accept that all the special effects were essential. To him, a good filmmaker could avoid special effects and still create drama and tension through suggestion.

My other example was Kurosawa's *Dream*. In one segment, he'd used CGI to create the illusion of a Van Gogh painting coming to life and a human character walking into that recreated, and now 3D, landscape. My father liked the film and had to accept that sequence could not have been made without the use of these expensive special effects. But then, he'd point out, the project had been financed by Hollywood bigwigs such as George Lucas and Steven Spielberg. While Kurosawa may have survived because of his reputation, any other filmmaker would have to succumb to their commercial pressure.

After many such arguments, we agreed that his case was not really against technology. At some point, even moving images had been considered the cutting edge of technology. Then a few creative people saw the potential of this technology to make artistic creations whose purpose was not so much to make money as it was to communicate. But I failed to convince him that creative artists would be able to take advantage of the newer technologies, and make meaningful cinema out of them one day. His mistrust of Hollywood and commercial Indian cinema was too deep; he simply could not accept that anyone could maintain their creative independence while using technology that was controlled by the big money that funded it. He would rather not be able to use the technology and find cheaper ways of achieving the same effect than risk losing his independence.

In *Mrigayaa*, there is a sequence where the protagonist is trying to hunt a deer with bow and arrow. He could not afford to shoot a real hunting scene with the deer and the hunter in the same shot. So, instead of creating a less-than-convincing scene, he tried to build it with suggestive close-ups and clever editing. It is hard to say what the effect would have been if he could have staged the scene for real, but the film did not suffer for that lack. That was his argument in support of innovative solutions and avoiding costly productions.

Looking at the Indian film scene today, I think he may have been correct after all. Many good films are being made whose technical quality far exceeds what could have been achieved in his era. I often wonder what could have happened if today's digital technologies were available to my father in the early seventies. He could have drastically lowered his production costs by shooting on small SLR cameras, and doing all his postproduction work at home using an inexpensive computer. Such technology is available now to all aspiring filmmakers, and there are many more intelligently made films today that are polished and thought-provoking. Yet, there is a tremendous paucity of Indian films that can create an impression in world cinema.

If we look at the three big film festivals in the world—Cannes, Berlin, Venice—I can barely find a single Indian film being included in the main competition sections over the last thirty years. Why is that so? I think the newer Indian films fail to surprise the world audience. They are all too carefully made. My father would have advised the new generation to spend less money—because that would let them take more chances. The official documentary film award at Cannes was awarded to two Indian documentaries in the last two years (2021 and 2022). This is probably proof that one can break new ground and surprise the audience when the commercial pressure is removed. These documentary filmmakers belong to the same creative environment and made something that surprised the world. But our feature films still cannot convince the selectors about their inclusion in the main competition section. I am sure there are some who are making interesting films outside the mainstream, but if so, why aren't those films getting more international exposure? Has something fundamentally changed since my father's time?

Many of the films my father made during the last thirty years of his career secured a place in the official selection of one of the major film festivals in the world. That does not imply they were all great films, but they must have surprised the festival selectors somehow. The most important criterion of excellence in any art is its ability to present something new in content or form. Of course, one can debate the validity of this yardstick, but he and many of his contemporaries managed to cross this steep barrier. However, since then, there has been a drought of such success. Perhaps my analysis of the root cause is a bit simplistic, and there may be many factors involved, but I have little doubt that a constant desire to recover the cost of an expensive production compromised the ability of subsequent filmmakers to take the necessary risks; without risk-taking, it is nearly impossible to surprise a discerning audience. The atmosphere of the film industry in India seems to be more in the grips of big money than ever before, and contemporary filmmakers are compelled to play by these rules. It may be easier said than done, but I hope a new generation of filmmakers will challenge that and start making low-cost films again and break new grounds that will surprise the world, just as Iranian films did a few decades ago.

UNKNOWN TONGUES

My father was a strictly bilingual person. Of course, he was most comfortable in Bengali, his mother tongue. He also grew up and spent his life in a middle-class Bengali atmosphere where most people around him were not comfortable speaking English. I think the same was true for him until he began travelling to national—and later international—festivals. His knowledge of English was acquired through his voracious reading habit, cultivated from his student days, and not because anyone spoke English around him.

Even though his written English was polished and sophisticated, he always spoke the language with a strong Bengali accent, and I have never seen any attempt to change that. Knowing him, I think he would not have felt comfortable adopting an accent that would make him appear very distant from his middle-class milieu. I faced a similar decision point when I moved to the US. Sometimes I had difficulty communicating with people on the street as they did not understand my heavily accented English. One remedy could have been to try and pick up the local accent; it would not have been that hard either. However, I made a conscious decision not to do so. I reasoned that I would still be perfectly understood among my usual US circle, the more educated population of academia, as they were already exposed to many different international accents. However, I felt that if I adopted an American accent, I would alienate myself from all the people I know in India.

Until recently, Bengalis had little reason to learn Hindi. That has changed recently through the proliferation of television and Hindi films and through greater cosmopolitanism. However, when I grew up, most of us never learnt Hindi beyond what was necessary to deal with street vendors. In my formative years, I watched a few Hindi films, and therefore had a slightly better understanding of the language, but for my father's generation, even that exposure was missing.

Yet, my father made eight films—almost a third of all his feature films—in languages other than Bengali. The percentage will be much higher if we include his short-length films, most of which were in Hindi. Given a choice, I think he would have made all his films in Bengali, but there were many factors that influenced his language choice, including finance, reaching a larger audience and access to a wider pool of actors.

He would often write the first idea for a film in English. Perhaps it was easier to share with his non-Bengali crew, potential financiers, friends, loan providers and his international connections. But his detailed screenplay was always in Bengali, irrespective of the final language of the film. If the film was to be made in a different language, then he had to rely on translators, and that was a major challenge.

For films like *Khandhar* (1983) or *Ek Din Achanak* (1989), even though the language was Hindi, the atmosphere my father was trying to build was essentially Bengali. This made it a little easier for him, since he knew the final target, so to speak. He also understood Hindi a little better than, say, Telugu. Nevertheless, he struggled to get the right translation. The translators he picked would not only know Bengali but also be familiar with Bengali culture. Despite which, many of them would translate his intentionally broken, half-finished Bengali sentences into complete, grammatically perfect Hindi sentences—and that he did not like. After the translation was done, he would run it by someone else to get a second or a third opinion and keep making changes. In the end, if he was using actors whom he trusted, the final review was done by the actors, and they always had the freedom to make more changes.

Sometimes the language was Hindi, but the cultural milieu was different from his familiar world. This happened in *Mrigayaa*, which was set in a Santhal tribal village during the British era. Even though he did not mix the language with Santhali, he tried to keep it culturally true and often consulted with village residents about the dialogues.

One day, they were shooting the scene where Mithun Chakraborty's character, a hunter, was to chase a deer. Mithun was asked to take aim and release his arrow. There was usually a crowd of locals watching; by then, they had learnt to stay silent while a shot was in progress. But that day, as Mithun was about to release his arrow, someone in the crowd made a disapproving sound. My father shouted, 'Cut!' and looked into the crowd for the person responsible. Since the others were pointedly staring at the culprit, he was not hard to spot. My father asked him why he'd made the sound. The man meekly said something; translated into Bengali, it meant that the Santhal people don't hold the arrow the way Mithun was holding it. The man said they didn't hold it using their index finger and thumb, as most of us are used to. In fact, they do not use the thumb at all. Instead, they hold the arrow and pull the string using the knuckles of the index and the middle finger. When asked why, he explained that it is because they were the descendants of Ekalavya, who had to sacrifice his thumb to his guru. My father was stunned by this explanation, by the idea that a Hindu mythological story could influence the behaviour of an entire population, and, of course, by its political implication.

For those who may not be familiar with this story from the Mahabharata, Ekalavya was a lower-caste archer who was as good as his upper-caste competitors. Yet, no upper-caste guru would take him on as a student. So, he created a clay statue of Drona, the greatest teacher of archery, and practised in front of it. One day, walking in the forest with his favourite student, Arjuna, Drona came across evidence of Ekalavya's skills. He asked Ekalavya who had taught him archery so well. Ekalavya bowed to Drona and said he himself was his teacher. Drona said that in order to be his student, Ekalavya must first pay his dues. Ekalavya replied that he would do anything to meet his obligation to his teacher. Drona asked for the thumb of his right hand, which Ekalavya readily cut off and presented to him.

Despite the loss of this essential finger, Ekalavya continued to practise and remastered his art.

Even though the people of this tribe probably predate the Mahabharata, somehow this story has got entwined with their tribal culture. They identify with that lower-caste hero and even adopt a style to imitate Ekalavya's loss of his thumb.

My father was very moved by it all.

Later, at an international festival, the screening of the film was followed by a press conference in the course of which my father shared this story. Afterwards, a European reporter approached him and said that he too was an amateur archer, and that most archers throughout the world never use the thumb. Releasing the bow using the thumb and the index finger introduces a slight asymmetry, which in turn can alter the trajectory of the arrow. A more effective method is to use the index and middle fingers, where the release is more symmetric.

To my father, it was a great story illustrating how myth can enter a culture and lend false meaning to an act. The Santhal people probably never used their thumb for practical reasons, but by incorporating this story into their history, they had added more meaning to their identity.

By the same token, we love to believe that indigenous people are still shrouded in their ancient myths. In reality, the younger generations know perfectly well how the 'real world' works. One evening, my father asked a group of young men about the ongoing drought, and whether there were any plans to perform the usual anti-drought ritual. He was clearly joking with them. One young man looked at him and said: What's the point of pleasing the gods up there when the real gods control the gates of the Massanjore Dam down in the valley? Perhaps we should invent a ritual to please them?

My father's first film in a different language was in Odia. *Matira Manisha* was based on a famous and very popular Odia novel by Kalindi Charan Panigrahi. It is the story of two rural brothers. The older is more respectful of the traditional ways and their father's desire not to split up their ancestral land, but the younger brother and his wife have different desires. To maintain peace, the older brother gives away all of their land to his brother. In the film, this rift between the two brothers, and the two different perspectives of life they represent, is not reconciled, and they go their different ways. This contrasts with the novel, where the younger brother understands his mistake and the two brothers get back together to lead a harmonious life.

My father tried to interpret the story in the context of his reality in which joint families were breaking down. He wanted to emphasize the inevitability of the split—and he had no regrets about it. But the general Odia audience was not happy to see an outsider, who did not understand the local culture, change the central moral of their favourite novel. My father was adamant about the ending. So the producer decided to create a different ending, more aligned with the original novel, and released a version without my father's name in the credits.

In those days, it was almost impossible to watch other regional films. Therefore, *Matira Manisha* was never shown in Calcutta except for a single screening by the Calcutta Film Society at the Academy of Fine Arts auditorium. There were only a few film societies in Calcutta in those early days, and everyone in the intelligentsia interested in serious cinema was a member of one of these two or three film societies. Since these screenings were the only way to watch regional films, they were very well attended. I remember going to the screening for *Matira Manisha*. To our utter surprise, we found the auditorium almost empty, and the few attendees seemed not to be the regular crowd. The film-society members, we later understood, had given their tickets to their domestic workers, who often hailed from Odisha and so of course spoke the language. Such was the chauvinism of the mainstream Bengalis in the sixties. An Odia film, even if made by someone they knew, was not worth watching simply because of the language. Bengali and Odia are not all that different. But the Bengalis of that era refused to accept that meaningful culture could come from a state other than West Bengal. I hope our attitudes have changed to some extent over the last fifty years, but I am not sure they are entirely transformed.

My father's first film to incorporate Hindi was *Bhuvan Shome*, along with several other languages. While the main film was in Hindi, some of the Saurashtrian characters mixed Gujarati with their Hindi. The main character, however, was a Bengali; he often used Bengali exclamations, and his inner thoughts were spoken in Bengali.

My father had to depend on his Hindi-speaking assistants heavily, as his own Hindi was atrocious.

Once, when he was staying with his Bombay-based assistant, Somendra Batra, in his bachelor's pad in Bandra, they were talking late into the night. Suddenly he told his host, 'Somen, chalo ghumne jayega'—Come, Somen, let's go out for a walk. Somen was surprised at that request at that rather late hour, but didn't want to question his boss. He went into the bathroom to change into his street clothes. When he came back, he found my father fast asleep! The confusion had been caused by my father's bad Hindi. He had used the Bengali word for sleeping ('ghum') and transformed it to 'ghumne'—going out—to make it sound like Hindi.

Language-wise, the most difficult was his Telugu film. This language has almost no similarity to Bengali, and he was essentially blind to the translation. As usual, he wrote his screenplay in Bengali and then found a Telugu-speaking writer, who'd lived in Calcutta for many years and spoke Bengali like a native, to translate it. My father was never a very trusting person when it came to his work, and he remained sceptical about the quality of the translation. When they arrived in Hyderabad, before leaving for the location in a village in Telengana, he spoke with a local literary person and requested him to go over the translation. The writer was very critical of it, and felt the translator had lived too long away from Andhra Pradesh and hence forgotten the nuances of the language. So the screenplay went through another round of translation.

When they reached the village in Telengana, my father, once again, wanted some local villagers to go over the dialogues. There was another round of significant changes as they found the second version too urban. However, there was one phrase they just could not make any sense of. My father had used a common Bengali expression for laziness, which compares a person to a water buffalo, because water buffalos spend a good part of their day half-submerged in water, doing nothing much but wallowing. The translator in Calcutta had no problem with the phrase, neither did the translator in Hyderabad. But the villagers protested—they saw no sense in calling a water buffalo lazy; for them it was an extremely hard-working animal, doing all the heavy lifting for them. My father removed the expression as soon as he realized it only made sense to an urban person who has a distorted view of the animal.

There were other problems he faced with the sound of the language. At one point, the woman in the film, pushed to extreme frustration by her husband and father-in-law, shouts back: 'No, no, no!' The word 'no' sounds similar in many languages around the world: na, nehi, non, niet, etc. In Telugu, however, it is 'ledu'. My father wanted the phonetic punch that 'no, no, no' or 'na, na, na' or 'nehi, nehi, nehi' has, and he felt that 'ledu, ledu, ledu' simply did not work. He asked the translators to find an alternative, but they failed to do so. Reluctantly, he agreed to 'ledu', but was extremely unhappy about it.

While my father agreed to work in different regions of India, he refused to make a film outside the country. There were a few offers and suggestions to make a film in Europe, but he did not feel comfortable with that at all—he felt he did not understand those cultures at a deep enough level to be able to capture them in a film. The most lucrative suggestion came from his friend, Colombian author Gabriel García Márquez. As an author, he was reluctant to allow people to adapt his books into films, but he said that if my father ever wanted to make a film out of a novel, he would agree. This was a great honour, and a sign of the confidence that Márquez had in my father's abilities. But my father promptly explained that he would not be able to do justice to any of his novels, as he simply did not have an intimate knowledge of Latin American life.

CASTING FOR FRESHNESS

My father started his film career with mostly established actors, but after *Bhuvan Shome* (1969), his choice of actors went through two more or less distinct phases. In the first, he wanted to use fresh faces whenever possible and did not care very much about their acting talents. He tried to either mentor them or cast other cinema tricks to hide their deficiencies. However, towards the latter third of his career, as he dealt with more complex subjects, his dependence on well-trained actors increased.

A film that my father desperately tried to disown all his life, *Raat Bhore* (1955), had Uttam Kumar, the biggest matinee idol Bengal has ever produced. I know nothing else about this film or how my father ended up casting him, or why the actor even agreed to work on a film by a complete newcomer. I don't think I will ever learn more, as no one alive seems to know about this film. I have seen a poster on the web, but that's about it. In 2022, I was attending an event at the Satyajit Ray Film Institute in Calcutta, celebrating my father's ninety-ninth birthday. There, Ashoke Viswanathan, a film scholar and the son of an actor my father worked with in the early sixties, narrated a story about this film. I am not sure about his source, but here's what he had to say:

Uttam Kumar, unlike many other film stars in India, was highly disciplined and had a strong work ethic. He was always on time.

One day, during the shooting of *Raat Bhore,* he was late arriving at the studio. Since this was highly unusual, and perhaps out of respect for the star, the crew decided to wait. He finally arrived a couple of hours later. Apologized for his tardiness. And then, almost as an afterthought, shared the reason for his delay—his mother had died that morning.

Hearing that story instantly reminded me of another incident in my life. I was a college student at the time, and a big fan of Badal Sircar, the most iconoclastic playwright and theatre director of that period. He did not believe in proscenium theatre, and used to stage his plays on street corners and often in a large hall in the Theosophical Society building. One day, I went to watch one of his plays with some of my friends. Sircar himself was acting. Once the play was over, someone from the group stepped up and made a brief statement: he was sad to inform the audience that a dear supporter of their group had died earlier that day—the wife of Badal Sircar!

There was stunned silence, and everyone was overwhelmed by the professionalism of the great playwright. I was sad too, but instead of being impressed, I saw the self-centred nature of celebrities. I would have respected him more if he had said he could not act that day because he had just lost his wife. That, to me, would have been the more honest and compassionate thing to do. That would have made him more human. I do not doubt that the performance was a painful one for him that day, but he could not resist the effect it would have on his audience in furthering the myth that was Badal Sircar.

Aside from *Raat Bhore,* my father mostly tried to stay away from actors who had already developed a certain screen persona and image. There was also the issue of keeping the cost low, which, as I've mentioned, he believed gave him greater creative freedom.

Our household laboured under a constant tension—because my father rarely cast my uncle Anup Kumar as an actor. I was very close to my uncle, so I used to be upset and embarrassed by that fact. But my father argued that since my uncle played so many comedic roles in popular films, the audience started laughing the moment they saw him on screen. He wanted to stay away from such overexposed and typecast actors.

The only well-known actors my father cat in his earlier films were Soumitra Chatterjee and Sabitri Chatterjee. Despite his growing popularity, Soumitra-kaka had the stature of an art-film actor because of all the films he made with Ray. He did not carry the baggage of a popular film star. Sabitri, on the other hand, was already very popular in commercial films, and I am not sure about the reason behind her selection; it could even have been at the insistence of his producer. My father worked with Soumitra again in the mid-sixties in *Akash Kusum* (1965), and then after a long gap, in the early nineties, in *Mahaprithibi*.

My father mostly preferred working with new faces, and in his second film, *Neel Akasher Neechey* (1958), he used Kali Banerjee to play a Chinese hawker.

In his third film, he cast a new actor who would eventually become one of the most respected faces in Bengali cinema. Madhabi Mukherjee played the role of a young wife in *Baishey Shravana* (1960). Her real name was Madhuri, but someone said 'Madhabi' would be a better screen name. Apparently someone else said she should have some dental work done to rectify a slight mis-alignment. Fortunately, she never paid attention; I believe it is one of those things that made her face so much more memorable. She eventually acted in several of Ritwik-kaka's films and is, of course, most remembered for her work with Ray.

Baishey Shravana was mostly shot on location in Barddhaman. I remember going there with my mother. I was five or six, and at some point, had to use the outhouse. Madhabi-di, a teenager herself, was asked to show me the way, and I remember the tremendous embarrassment that caused me. Almost fifty years later, when she was visiting Chicago, I asked her if she remembered that incident. I was relieved to know she did not, as it was a far less memorable incident for her than it was for a young five-year-old boy.

Soumitra played the male lead in three out of his next four films, including *Akash Kusum* (1965). In it, my father also cast a young actor, Aparna Sen, as the female lead. She was the daughter of his friend Chidananda Dasgupta, an advertising executive by profession but also one of the key founders of the film society movement in Calcutta. Aparna, when she was sixteen, first acted in Ray's *Teen Kanya*. She went on to become not only a very popular actor but also one of the most important contemporary filmmakers in India.

My father's next film, *Bhuvan Shome*. The technical crew was composed almost entirely of newcomers, mostly FTII graduates, and the five principal characters were all played by actors who were new to the film audience. Bhuvan Shome, a middle-aged railway executive, was played by his old friend and theatre personality, Utpal Dutt who received the National Award for Best Actor for this role. In time, he became a popular face in many commercial Hindi and Bengali films. Other roles were played by Shekhar Chatterjee, a theatre actor from Calcutta; Sadhu Meher, a brilliant actor from FTII; and Rochak Pandit, another theatre actor.

The young village girl was played by Suhasini Mulay, daughter of Vijaya Mulay, a documentary filmmaker and head of the Children's Film Society. My father had seen Suhasini as a teenager and wanted to cast her in this role. Her mother agreed, but Suhasini was getting ready for her high-school final exam. Other than modelling for an advertising films, she had no acting experience. But she was a confident and intelligent young woman, and that came across in the spontaneity with which she played her role. Despite her tremendous success, she decided not to pursue acting and went off to Canada for her higher studies. Later, after her return to India, she worked with both Ray and my father as an assistant director and then went on to make documentary films.

The film started with a voice-over introducing Bhuvan Shome. My father picked a tall young man who'd come home a few times in the hope of working with my father. My father had later considered him for *Ek Adhuri Kahani* too, but changed his mind; he thought the young man looked too distinguished to play a lower-middle-class character. This time, the young man's baritone would be perfect for the voice-over. The young actor had just been cast in his first film role in Khwaja Ahmad Abbas', *Saat Hindustani*. My father asked permission from Abbas, and paid the actor three hundred rupees for his work. That was the first film-related earning for Amitabh Bachchan, the person who would eventually become the most popular name in commercial Hindi cinema. He preferred to use only 'Amitabh' in the credits; in those days, it was considered unwise to use one's full name in commercial films since the last name could identify the person's regional identity. Fortunately, that convention slowly broke down, and actors were accepted nation-wide despite their local origins.

In my father's next film, *Interview* (1970), he cast several new faces, most notably, Ranjit Mallick. Ranjit had no acting experience and was noticeably nervous. We lived in the flat on Motilal Nehru Road then, which was also the venue for the first day of shooting. The scene required Ranjit to climb up our stairs, press the doorbell, wait a few seconds and then press it again and gradually get impatient at no one opening the door. A nervous Ranjit completely lost his sense of timing; instead of waiting a reasonable time, he pressed the button once and almost immediately pressed it again. My father got furious and started scolding him. That made Ranjit even more nervous, resulting in more mistakes. We all felt sorry for the new actor, but there was nothing we could do.

In another sequence where the character is having an angry outburst, Ranjit was incorrectly using one form of the *r* sound instead of another, both of which are used in Bengali. My father tried to correct him repeatedly, but Ranjit simply could not get it right. This made my father furious, and he started scolding him. By then, Ranjit was a little more familiar with my father's reactions, and in frustration, retorted, 'Can't a person mix up the two *r*'s when they are angry?'

Despite his struggles, the result was excellent, and Ranjit won the Best Actor award that year at the Karlovy Vary International Film Festival. He eventually became a very popular hero and acted in a vast number of Bengali films.

In *Interview*, Ranjit's mother was played by Karuna Banerjee, who had played the mother in Ray's Apu Trilogy. *Interview* intentionally mixed up fiction and reality. Ranjit played a character called Ranjit; at one point, he faces the camera and says that everything in the film is real, except his mother who is played by an actor, though she behaves in the same way as his real mother. At that point, we see a clip from *Pather Panchali* where Sarbojaya, played by Karuna Banerjee, breaks down while telling her husband about their daughter's death.

In *Ek Adhuri Kahani*, my father cast two completely new faces: Vivek Chatterjee and Arati Bhattacharya. Arati was introduced to my father by his still photographer, Nemai Ghosh.

My father's next film, *Calcutta 71* (1972), was a collection of several disjointed episodes connected by the theme of poverty and exploitation. In one of those episodes, he cast Madhabi Mukherjee after a gap of ten years. The other significant cast choice was of a theatre actor who had not acted in films for over two decades—my mother, Gita Sen. My parents met through her early acting career in theatre and films, but she stopped after they were married. I have never been able to discover why, but perhaps my birth had something to do with it. When I was about twelve, she returned to the theatre, acting in Utpal Dutt's productions at Minerva Theatre. This continued until 1971 when political unrest in the city forced her to stop. Right then, my father started to shoot *Calcutta 71* and asked her to play the widowed mother of a village boy who makes a living by smuggling rice to the city at a time when the rice supply and sales were controlled by the state. I think that little role again proved to the audience the quality and depth of her acting. That was also when, I think, my father fully realized the potential that was being wasted at home; since then, he tried hard to find ways to use her talent.

In *Padatik* (1973), he cast Dhritiman Chatterjee, already a friend as well as the lead in Ray's *Pratidwandi*, released a couple of years earlier. My father had tremendous respect for Dhritiman's intellectual depth and wanted him to play the lead in what was the most introspective film in his Calcutta Trilogy. He cast Dhritiman in several of his later films too. For the female lead, he chose a powerful veteran actor from Bombay, Simi Garewal. He must have seen her in Ray's *Aranyer Din Ratri*, and wanted her to play the sophisticated advertising executive who has given shelter to the political-activist character. He simply could not think of a local actor who could carry off the dignity, sophistication and complexity of that role.

In *Mrigayaa* (1976), he returned to newcomers. The lead male role, that of a tribal hunter, was played by a fresh FTII graduate. Mithun Chakraborty's personal style and attire were diametrically opposite to the role he was to play. Every time he visited us, he wore tight bell-bottomed trousers and a skin-fitting shirt left open halfway down his torso to expose his extremely well-built physique. One evening, I had to pick up some medicine from a neighbourhood pharmacy, and Mithun accompanied me. The store clerk, who knew me well, took a quick look at him and then asked me in a low voice who he was. Mithun was very much out of place in our typical middle-class milieu. However, it did not take too long for the transformation to begin. Just before leaving for their location in the tribal belt, the make-up team gave him a brutal haircut. Mithun looked as though he would die of grief, but he survived and ultimately went on to win the Best Actor Award from the Indian government that year. Later he became a huge star in Bombay and was dubbed the 'disco king'.

In the same film, the female lead was to be played by Mamata Shankar, daughter of the dancers Uday and Amala Shankar, niece of Ravi Shankar and sister of Ananda Shankar who composed the music for many of my father's films. Mamata had never acted before, but when my father approached her and her mother, they agreed to give it a try. I was a college student then, and I, along with all my male friends, were stunned by her beauty and charmed by her dancer's grace. Every time she visited us, I would stare at her in awe but could never pluck up enough courage to talk to her. One day, just before they were supposed to leave for their location, she unexpectedly came up to me, held my arm and pulled me towards the little balcony outside our living room. My heart almost stopped. Once we were away from the crowd, she asked me for a favour: while she would be shooting in Massanjore, could I some-how smuggle letters from her boyfriend without letting her mother know? Her mother would be going with her on the shoot. Alas, it was not a romantic rendezvous but my demotion to the role of messenger. Mamata also became a very well-respected actor in Bengali cinema, and, during her long career, worked with all the major filmmakers in the region.

Mamata also acted in his next Telugu-language film, *Oka Oorie Katha* (1977). Her character's father-in-law was played by veteran actor Vasudev Rao, well known for his role in B. V. Karanth's *Chomana Dudi*. I have never met him, but everyone at the shoot, including my father, was stunned by the depth of his talent, his dedication and his uncompromised devotion to the role he was playing. He never took off his tattered and dirty costume, even when he was not in front of the camera.

In my father's next film, *Parashuram* (1978), he cast Arun Mukherjee, director and lead actor of the Bengali play on which the film was based, to play the main role of a displaced farmer who now leads a homeless existence in the city. The other role, that of a homeless woman, was played by another new actor, Sreela Majumdar. My mother used to listen to radio plays on the only Bengali radio station of those days. She had been impressed by a voice-actor and mentioned it to my father. It was Sreela. It was easy to spot her talent, and she worked in many of his later films. It is a shame that even though she won the national award for that role, she could never fully break into mainstream Bengali cinema, the most likely cause being her dark complexion. Seventy-five years after freedom from colonial rule, we still equate beauty with fair skin.

My father's success with introducing new acting talents was a mixed one. Many became well established and critically acclaimed, while others failed to make a mark. The same probably applies to Ray. The only Indian filmmaker I can think of who has been able to introduce new and remarkable actors consistently is Shyam Benegal.

CASTING FOR EXPERIENCE

In the next phase of his career, the types of films my father made changed in significant ways. His enemy was no longer outside— he was more interested in pointing the finger at his own milieu and self. This introspective phase also required more complex stories, which in turn needed more experienced actors.

This phase began with *Ek Din Pratidin* (1979). About a night when the breadwinner of a lower-middle-class family fails to come back home on time. He needed a powerful cast to hold that claustrophobic atmosphere together, and went back to some of his favourite female actors—Sreela Majumdar, Mamata Shankar and my mother.

My father initially offered the role of the mother to another great theatre actor, Tripti Mitra. She wanted to know the relative importance of the role compared with her two daughters, played by Mamata and Sreela. That gave my father pause, and he refused to give her a clear answer. Therefore, she decided to decline. Later, after watching the film, she commented that she was glad she refused, for then we would not have seen the brilliant performance by Gita Sen. I think she was right.

Akaler Shandhaney (1980) was perhaps one of his most complex films, at least structurally speaking. Even the relationships between the various characters were extremely complex. Once again, he had to depend on powerful actors such as Smita Patil, Dhritiman Chatterjee, my mother and his director-friend Rajen Tarafdar. Rajen, who was not a professional actor, surprised everyone with his remarkable portrayal. Smita, on the other hand, was already one of the most well-respected actors in the world of parallel cinema. My father was extremely happy with her sensitive portrayal of herself in that film-within-a-film. The only problem was her Bengali accent. He did not want the unnecessary distraction of making her character a non-Bengali. He tried to use her voice but was not happy with her accent. Eventually, he used another Bengali actor to dub her voice. Rightly so, Smita was not happy about this decision, and I believe he should have tried a little harder. It is very hard for any good actor to see that her spoken words are no longer her own.

In *Chalchitra* (1981), he finally did something he always wanted to do—he cast my mother in a lead role. She played a widow. Her son was played by another theatre actor who had never acted in cinema, Anjan Dutt. His was an upcoming name in Calcutta's English- language theatre scene. It was an odd choice— Anjan was quite anglicized and removed from the lower-middle-class character he was to play. However, this was the beginning of a long relationship between the Anjan and my father. Anjan later mentioned that this experience changed him profoundly as an individual as it did his relationship with Calcutta. In 2022, he announced he was making of a film based on that transformative experience between a young actor and his director.

My father's relationship with Anjan extended far beyond that of an actor and a director. Gradually, an intellectual trust developed between them. Despite their differences in lifestyle and politics and even aesthetic viewpoints, they respected each other. Anjan eventually contributed as a writer and executive producer to many of my father's later projects. As Anjan himself became a film director, my father took a deep interest in Anjan's films. My father was not thrilled by Anjan's more commercially motivated ones, and I think Anjan did not want my father to watch them either. But they often talked about Anjan's serious films.

In my opinion, *Chalchitra* remains the best example of my mother's acting talent. The audience, especially in India, tends to appreciate a piece of acting when the character is thrown into a dramatic and unusual situation. Even actors find it easier to perform such roles. It is far more difficult to portray a character to whom nothing unusual happens. My mother did a remarkable job of playing an unremarkable woman, simply living her life. Of course, I am biased, but I doubt any other actor available to my father at that time could have played it better.

In his next film, *Kharij* (1982), he cast Anjan, Mamata and Sreela in a tense story about the death of a servant boy and its consequences. By then, all three were trained actors. The superb acting helped create the film's atmosphere, winning it the Special Jury Prize at Cannes. More than forty years later—at the time of this writing—another filmmaker, Kaushik Ganguly, is making a film called *Palan*, the name of the servant boy in *Kharij*. We will see the same three actors playing the same roles as in *Kharij*, but now forty years older.

Next, my father took up *Khandhar* (1983), something far more internal and introspective than anything he had done before. He knew from the start that he would need the best actors he could find. It was based on an iconic Bengali story by Premendra Mitra, so the natural choice was to make the film in Bengali. However, my father failed to find the actors he was looking for and decided to do it in Hindi so that he could cast actors like Shabana Azmi and Naseeruddin Shah. He also cast brilliant actors like Pankaj Kapoor and Annu Kapoor, plus some of his other favourites—

Sreela Majumdar, Rajen Tarafdar and my mother. I think it is one of his most well-acted films, and it would not have worked if the acting quality was anything less than stellar.

In *Khandhar*, my mother played the role of a bedridden, blind woman. It was a difficult role, for she could only rely on facial expressions and voice. She did an excellent job, but when it came to her voice, her Hindi accent was far from perfect. For anyone else, I am certain that my father would have used a Hindi-speaking actor to dub, as he did with Smita Patil in *Akaler Shandhaney*. But this is where his respect towards my mother came through, and he allowed her to keep her voice despite the strong accent. My father did not know enough Hindi to realize that her accent was faulty, but the other actors around him, like Shabana and Naseeruddin, could have warned him. They didn't, and insisted he keep my mother's voice, and he did.

In his next multinational production, *Genesis* (1986), he returned to the best acting trio he could find. In that modern-day fable, Naseeruddin Shah and Om Puri played the farmer and the weaver, respectively, while Shabana Azmi played the woman who drifts between them. Based on some press interviews, Naseeruddin was not happy with the film or his role and mentioned that he did not even care to watch the finished product. I am unsure what prompted that reaction, as was my father. Many years later, when Naseeruddin called my father about something else, my father asked him about his earlier reaction. I don't clearly remember what Naseeruddin said, but whatever it was, he admitted his reaction had been excessive, and he apologized for his outburst.

Working with very talented actors always comes with a risk. Unlike novices, they have strong opinions about the validity of the character they are to play. Naseeruddin must not have felt comfortable with the logic of his character, and my father must have failed to convince him. *Genesis* was an unusual film, as it was more of a fable than a real-life drama. Does that excuse it from not following the usual logic of character development and interpersonal psychology? That is a hard question to answer, but clearly, Naseeruddin and my father had different views about it.

Shabana was back in his next film, *Ek Din Achanak* (1989), playing the eldest daughter of a professor who goes missing. It is probably the most intellectually autobiographical film my father made, in which he addressed the issue of personal mediocrity. No matter how successful we appear to the external world, we all must feel the crisis of mediocrity deep within and the profound regret that we live just once. Shabana understood this at a very personal level, and mentioned somewhere that it remains one of the most satisfying roles in her acting career.

In *Mahaprithibi*, my father returned to Soumitra Chatterjee after a relatively long gap. The rest of the cast comprised strong actors—Aparna Sen, Victor Banerjee, Anjan Dutt and my mother. Gone were the days when he would pick someone off the street to play the main role. He only wanted to work with seasoned actors then, but was still careful not to pick someone who would come with a predetermined audience expectation.

In *Antareen* (1993), he surprised everyone by casting Dimple Kapadia, a name associated with glamorous Hindi films. She played a mysterious and lonely woman confined to a posh, high-rise flat. The other character was played by Anjan Dutt—an author, temporarily living in a dilapidated mansion. The two never meet; the only communication between them is through occasional phone calls. At the end, there is a possibility of a meeting but that fades away, leaving the two lonely souls isolated in a crowded world. My father justified his choice of Dimple because of her face, which he believed was the personification of loneliness and melancholy.

In my father's last film, *Amar Bhuvan* (2002), also a fable of sorts, he desperately tried to discover an island of humanity and profound goodness in a world being destroyed by war and hatred.

For the first time, he worked with Nandita Das, whom he had admired for many years. Nandita remained very close to my father till the very end. There was a kind of tenderness in their relationship that went far beyond professional friendship.

Once, my father was in hospital after a hip surgery and feeling particularly vulnerable. He was not in good shape, and that made him cranky and harder to manage. Nisha and I had to take turns visiting Calcutta and taking care of my ageing parents. It was Nisha's turn to be there, and she was in hospital with my father. At one point, Nandita showed up; she never missed visiting my parents whenever she came to the city. Since Nandita was there, Nisha took the opportunity to step away from his bedside to take care of something else. When she returned, she could see from the doorway that Nandita was trying to feed him. The moment was so tender that she decided not to disturb it and allowed them to cherish that beautiful moment.

He never made another film, but I am certain that if he did, he would have found a way to cast Nandita again. He had a special kind of confidence in a few of his female actors, like Shabana, Smita, Nandita, Sreela, my mother. He would not have to explain what he wanted but simply have a conversation, sometimes on an entirely different topic, to convey the desired emotional state. He knew that once the emotion was conveyed, they could do the rest, including changing the actions and the dialogue when necessary.

THE CREW

During his fifty-year-long career, my father worked with many people, and it would be hard for me to talk about all of them, but I would like to mention a few that influenced him in one way or another.

Up until *Akash Kusum*, his cinematographer was Sailaja Chatterjee, a bespectacled, intense-looking, small-statured person. To his friends, he was known as 'Paul', an unusual nickname for someone who grew up in a small town in East Bengal when the state was not yet divided. Paul-kaka, as I used to call him, had some fascinating stories to share. When he was in his late teens, he'd joined the armed faction of the freedom movement then labelled as 'terrorists' by the British administration. On one occasion, they were trying to loot a post-office vault for money and other valuables in order to fund their operations, but something went wrong, and the colonial police captured many of them.

Paul-kaka was injured and woke up in a big room full of hospital beds. He knew the hospital because his father was a doctor there—a loyalist who unequivocally disapproved of his son's association with the freedom movement. In fact, they had stopped talking to each other. Paul-kaka's immediate fear was that he might have to face his father in that condition. A little later, he saw his father making rounds through that huge room, checking each patient. Finally, he came to Paul-kaka's bed, looked at his wounds but did not make eye contact. But just before moving on to the next bed, he said in a low voice that he was considering quitting his job at the government hospital.

Decades later, in *Padatik*, in the last sequence, the revolutionary character who was in hiding meets his father next to the bedside of his dead mother. The father, who never agreed with his son's politics, wanted to say something important. He told his son that he refused to sign the papers his company had asked him to, agreeing to refrain from joining a union strike. The father touched the son's shoulder and said, 'Go, be brave.' I have a strong conviction this memorable sequence reflected the story that my father heard from his friend.

Paul-kaka was then imprisoned in the penal colony that the British constructed in the Andaman Islands. It was a brutal place, separated by hundreds of miles of ocean from the mainland of India. Most people did not survive it, but Paul-kaka was released when the country achieved independence a few years later. I am not sure how he ended up becoming a cinematographer, but he eventually managed to carve out a career with a decent income.

Almost fifteen years after earning his freedom, he was going home in a taxi one day. He noticed the taxi driver looking at him in his rearview mirror, but didn't pay much attention. After paying his fare, he got off and started walking towards his home. Just then, he heard the driver uttering a name he hadn't heard in decades— the secret name he'd used during his 'terrorist' days. He turned around and immediately recognized the man—he'd been part of their group, one of those who'd escaped arrest on that final operation. The man begged Paul-kaka to accompany him to his house as he had something very important to share; he had been waiting for this encounter for a very long time. Paul-kaka got back in the taxi, and they drove to the driver's home in a dingy part of South Calcutta. The whole family lived in a single, shabby room. After some talk, the driver asked his wife and children to leave them alone for a bit. Then he rummaged through an old trunk and fished out an old biscuit tin. He told Paul-kaka that he had been holding on to this box since the day of their last raid, but hadn't known what to do with it. When he opened the box, Paul-kaka found it contained a handful of gold jewellery they had stolen from the post-office vault. Through all his years of poverty, he had never considered selling them to make ends meet.

Another person from my father's early days was Indore Sen. He assisted my father in many of his early films and acted as my babysitter when needed. Known more by his nickname, Chandu, he was a formidable cricketer. It was not uncommon in those days for someone to organize a cricket match within the film fraternity to raise funds for some cause. The crowds bought tickets to see the film stars play cricket. During those matches, where gameplay was not all that important, Chandu-kaka was the one serious player, and whichever team he was on was sure to win the match. At some point, he started making his own films, many of which were commercially successful. I am not sure why he gradually drifted away from our home, but there was no contact except for when we bumped into him at some public event. There was no animosity, no conflict—my father and he simply drifted apart. I never understood why.

Another long-time associate was Gangadhar Naskar, who was his editor in almost half of his films. The role of an editor in the kind of films my father or Ray made was somewhat different from that of an editor in commercial cinema. Right or wrong, these directors gave very little creative freedom to their editors—they preferred to do their own editing, and the editor's role became more technical than creative. This was the case for Gangadhar Naskar.

My father would sit like a hawk over his shoulder, tense and alert, and dictate every single cut.

One day, I was visiting his editing room at New Theatres Studio and witnessed an exchange between them. Ganga-kaka had just finished cutting and joining two adjacent scenes, and my father and he were watching the result again. My father was unhappy and claimed the cut to be a little longer than he'd requested. Ganga-kaka protested, saying it was exactly what my father had wanted. My father asked him to play it again, and to stop exactly when he slapped Ganga-kaka's back. He did so, and put a pencil mark on the exact frame. My father, for some reason, asked him to roll it back and play it again. Ganga-kaka did, and again stopped as soon as my father slapped his back. Another mark was put in. My father repeated it a third time and then asked Ganga-kaka to take the film out of the machine and look for the three marks. All three marks were exactly on the same frame, two or three frames shorter than the original cut. They smiled at each other, and the extra frames were taken out.

The usual practice of editing in those days was to cut the film with scissors, scrape off the film emulsions on both strips, apply a liquid cement using a brush, then manually join them together, making sure the strips and the sprockets were perfectly straight and aligned. It required considerable skill to align them correctly, which all editors had. Then a simple manual tool came into the antiquated editing rooms of the city—a splicer. Here one had to position the two film strips on opposite sides of a sprocketed bed, place clear adhesive tape on top of the strips, then close the lid to create a perfect join. It was precise and quick, with the added benefit that no frames were lost in the process. When my father insisted that Ganga-kaka use this little gadget, he refused, saying he could do just as well with his hands. Perhaps this was the beginning of the end of their relationship. In his next film, my father started working with a younger editor who had just graduated from FTII. Mrinmoy Chakraborty remained his editor for the next several films until his sudden and untimely death.

My father's make-up artist for many years was Debi Haldar, a man who continued to dress in his white dhoti and shirt, even when it became a seriously outdated dressing convention. Debi-kaka's dedication and love for the film team were exemplary. Every time a film would get a theatrical release, one could find him in front of the theatre every evening, trying to catch the reaction of the audience coming out of the afternoon show.

Another person I remember from my youngest days was a production assistant called Gokul. He was a man of very short stature and as dark as an Indian could get. Gokul-da was sometimes paid extra to babysit me when my mother would go off to perform at Minerva Theatre. Trying to keep me entertained and engaged, he would concoct tall tales of his shooting adventures. Sometimes it would be a struggle with alligators while shooting near a river; on other days, a battle with bandits who had come to steal production properties. Gokul-da was a powerful hero in my life.

Even in real life, Gokul-da had heroic qualities. While shooting *Matira Manisha* in rural Odisha, the film team had built mud huts with thatched roofs. One evening, a heavy storm threatened to blow away the roof of one hut. Suddenly everyone noticed that Gokul-da had climbed up on its roof and sprawled out on top of it to hold it down against the heavy gale. Another time, my mother and I accompanied the team to South India when my father was making a long documentary on the history of India. It was an incredibly hot summer afternoon when they were shooting an old stone temple in Tanjore. Suddenly it started raining, so we all rushed back to the van, and the van headed back to our hotel down a rural road. The back door of the van was open, and rainwater was soaking us. Suddenly, Gokul-da decided to open a very large garden umbrella originally used to shade the camera during a shoot. That heroic act almost pulled the little man out of the van, but he was saved when the others made him release his grip on the umbrella. Gokul-da died young, perhaps as a result of excessive drinking and a reckless lifestyle.

Another amazing member of my father's team was his long-time production manager, Mukul Chowdhury. Mukul-babu was the epitome of quiet efficiency. Always clad in his starched white dhoti and kurta, he did not talk much and did not speak English—which is an essential skill to operate within the Indian bureaucracy—but could solve any problem. I remember, during the shooting of *Mrigayaa*, a scene had to be shot at Calcutta's sprawling British-era Tollygunge Club. The club manager, Robert Wright, was playing the role of the English administrator and agreed to allow use of the club grounds. Suddenly, the evening before the shoot, my father decided he wanted to show a deer that the tribal character had caught and brought to the British administrator. Anyone who knows Calcutta will know it is not the kind of place where one can easily find a deer. However, Mukul-babu was not perturbed. He listened to the request, nodded and went away. The next morning, he arrived at the club with a live deer. None of us knew where he got it from. Unfortunately, the deer died at the end of the day—perhaps out of stress or dehydration. Everyone was devastated and regretted that they did not have a proper animal handler. We never did come to know how Mukul-babu pulled it off.

On another occasion, my father sent me to the passport office when he suddenly realized that his passport had expired, and he had to travel abroad soon. I filled out all the necessary forms and went to the government office and waited for my turn behind hundreds of other applicants. There was complete chaos, as there was no organized queue. I was rapidly losing hope that I would ever be able to submit the application. Suddenly, I saw Mukul-babu. He was annoyed that I had been sent to do such an important task. He took the forms from me and then marched to the gate that separated the crowd from the counter. The guard at the gate tried to stop us. Mukul-babu frowned with deep annoyance and almost scolded the man. He said he had important business and simply walked in with me. The work was done in a matter of minutes. I still don't understand what his magic was.

The team member with whom Bondhu had the deepest relationship was his cinematographer who had worked with him since *Bhuvan Shome*, K. K. Mahajan. They were very different in nature. Mahajan-kaka spoke very little, drank heavily and had a rough exterior. Yet, the relationship between them was tender and loving. They understood each other perfectly, and Mahajan-kaka could instantly sense what my father was looking for and always delivered. In situations where photographic precision was secondary and just getting the shot done was important, Mahajan-kaka was ready to take on the challenge. I have seen him get into the trunk of a moving car, into the battery compartment below a train car right next to the wheels, lean forward from the rooftop wall of a highrise building, or run through narrow lanes where his only vision was through the camera lens. For many Calcutta street scenes, they would let the actors go into the crowd before the shot and then suddenly leave their car with the camera in hand and start shooting. There was no detailed planning, no light measurement, and of course, no lights or reflectors. This way, Mahajan-kaka could finish the shot even before the crowd realized a film was being shot.

Mahajan-kaka suffered from advanced cancer and, towards the end, could not talk and had to communicate through writing. In 2013, when my father wrote the book on his personal hero, Charlie Chaplin, he dedicated the book to his friend, Mahajan:

In memory of

K. K. Mahajan

My cameraman (1969–1989), who died of cancer.

When he looked through my camera for the first time—
and that was his first feature film—I asked him to remember
the quote from Niels Bohr, the iconic physicist:
Confidence comes from not only being always right,
but also from not fearing to be wrong.

K. K. is dead, I am still alive.

Subrata Mitra, the cinematographer who worked with Ray for all of his initial films, was just the opposite. Subrata-kaka was a perfectionist. Everything he did was meticulously planned, and the results were uniformly spectacular. My father and Subrata-kaka were close friends. Ray moved on from him, as working with such a compulsive perfectionist was becoming difficult for him. My father often toyed with the idea of working with Subrata-kaka but backed out at the last moment because he realized their approaches to filmmaking were so different that frequent conflicts would be inevitable, possibly destroying their friendship. Subrata-kaka rented out his camera equipment, and my father always tried to use his camera, as it was the best maintained in the industry. Subrata-kaka's brother Bachchu was the caretaker of the equipment and was as careful and fussy as his older brother. During the filming of *Bhuvan Shome*, they had to shoot a lot in the sand dunes of Saurashtra. There was sand everywhere, which made Bachchu-da extremely nervous about his machine. Since he could not stop the work, every evening, after coming back to their camp, when everyone else rested, Bachchu-da would spread out a white bedsheet and dismantle the camera part by part and clean each component using his fine brush and air bulb, and then reassemble the whole thing.

Subrata-kata started adding sound equipment to his rental business with Nagra tape recorders and specialized microphones, and took the same interest in sound that he took in photography when he made *Pather Panchali*. During the making of *Calcutta 71*, my father asked him if he could be his sound recordist. To cut costs, he decided to record his music not in a sound studio but in the auditorium of Goethe-Institut/Max Muller Bhavan. During the two days of recording, the musicians were asked to set up their orchestra on the stage. Subrata-kata created his recording station by setting up a table in the middle of the auditorium. As expected, he made them turn off the air-conditioner as well as all the fans to eliminate the hum. But Subrata-kaka was still not happy and, with his headphones on, kept complaining about the sound of some machine. No one else could hear anything. My father borrowed his headphones and could hear nothing either. When my father told him that it was his imagination, Subrata-kaka, using a highly directional long microphone, pointed in the direction of the sound. They eventually figured out that there was a small hay-cutting shop on the other side of the street, and it was that sound that Subrata-kaka was picking up. They had to pay to have the machine stopped during their recording session. But that was not the end of it. Subrata-kaka took hours to set up the microphones on stage, and the professional musicians were getting impatient. At one point, Subrata-kaka handed his headphone to my father to listen—he could hear the musicians using extremely foul language about their amateur sound recordist, not knowing that the carefully placed microphones were picking it up and delivering it straight into the ears of the recordist himself!

During my college days, I formed a wonderful relationship with Subrata-kaka. I had a passion for electronics and engineering in general, and he appreciated that. He would spend hours describing the technical details of his favourite machines. This turned into a rare trust, and he would allow me to see and touch some of his precious collections in their dilapidated home on Lansdowne Road. There are many stories to be told there, but this is probably not the place. Now that both the brothers are gone, I often wonder what happened to all those machines. Every time I visit the city, I see their red-brick house, still standing but in ruins.

Despite my father's deepest trust in Mahajan-kaka, he also wanted to work with other cinematographers from time to time. For *Parashuram*, he worked with a new FTII graduate, Ranajit Roy, but for just one film. I can no longer recall whether my father chose to work with Ranajit because he wanted to try something different or because Mahajan-kaka was busy with other projects in Bombay. However, after that, my father came back to Mahajan-kaka until he worked on *Genesis*. That was an international production, and the producers preferred to work with a European cinematographer, Carlo Varini.

In *Mahaprithibi*, he asked another young person to do his camera work—Sashi Anand, who went on to be his cinematographer for the next few films. Sashi also composed the music for *Antareen*.

In my father's final film, *Amar Bhuvan* (2002), he worked with a very talented cinematographer who had already made a name for himself. My father came to know Avik Mukhopadhyay through the films of Rituparno Ghosh and Aparna Sen, and felt that Avik could create the light that my father was envisioning for that film. I remember my father wrote to me about a certain kind of light he had seen in the paintings of Rembrandt. He wanted the faces in that film to have an inner glow that was common in Rembrandt's portraits; he asked me to find some of those images and send them to him so that he could share them with his new cinematographer.

There was always a still photographer in the production team who not only took the film stills used for advertising and promotion but also chronicled the process. I can think of two such people. During the early seventies, it was Nemai Ghosh, who was also part of Ray's team. Just before he started shooting *Padatik* in 1973, an unknown young photographer stopped by our place and showed my father some of his work. Perhaps due to his bias towards new talents, he suddenly decided to switch and Subhash Nandy got the job.

Subhash-da used to be a helping hand in a photographic studio, which happened to belong to the father of a classmate of mine. While working there, he learnt to work in the darkroom. Only much later, he finally got his hands on a camera and started taking pictures. Starting with *Padatik*, he was my father's still photographer until his last film. He built a successful career, but it all collapsed through several mishaps. Towards the end, he was in deep financial difficulty. Once, he wrote to me saying that he had the task of shooting one of my father's later films but could not tell Bondhu that he had no camera to shoot with, since all his equipment was stolen from his studio. I gave him my camera so that he could continue. Despite his tremendous talent, he did not have the skills to market himself well. Subhash-da died very young, and today people hardly know of him.

There are many other names that come to mind. There was the eccentric but brilliant production designer Biswakalyan, who could manage to get drunk early in the morning but still deliver. There was my father's old-time artist-friend, Khaled Chowdhury, who created a scale model of a castle for *Chorus* from which the mythical industrial power tried to control everything. There were my father's reliable film assistants, Bidyut Bhattacharya and Amal Sarkar. There was Supantha, who had the keenest eye to fill all the smaller acting roles. There were a host of production assistants whose dedication and hard work always amazed me—Jitesh-babu, Bishu, Himadri, Nitin, and too many others to name. Filmmaking is a collective effort. Without any one of these people, the films that they made would not have been the same.

MUSIC

If one looks at the list of music directors in my father's films, a pattern will emerge. He never stayed with the same composer for more than two or three films. Usually, he used them for a single film. I can identify two reasons for this. One, he did not have a cultivated taste in music. Not that he did not like some music, but it was not something he was passionate about, and therefore never studied it. Two, he did not like too much music in his films. He preferred the sounds of the environment and silence over a sound-track saturated with music. Of course, it is possible that these are not isolated reasons, and his lack of a cultivated musical sense conditioned him to use music sparingly. Or it could be that he did not want too much music for the same reason he disliked sentimentalism of any kind. He wanted to touch his audience through reason, and not through emotional cracks. Music in a film has the power to emotionally prepare and sensitize the viewer. That makes it easier for the director to convey their ideas, for the audience's mind by then is ready to accept anything. My father never wanted to do that, and preferred his audience to be alert but not emotionally compromised.

My father always went to Hemanta Mukherjee for his earliest films, and the songs Mukherjee created for *Neel Akasher Neechey* are still favourites among Bengali listeners. Yet, my father always cringed at their sentimentality and never had any emotional attachment to them. I never saw a nostalgic look on his face when those songs were played over the loudspeakers in local puja pandals, which happened quite often. He never again used a song, except a thematic folk song in *Chorus* and in his last film, where he used a full Rabindrasangeet played on the radio.

He worked with well-known music directors like Sudhin Dasgupta in his earlier films, but the usage was sparse. Incidentally, I was the private tutor of Sudhin Dasgupta's son when I was in college; I also tutored the daughter of Utpal Dutt for a while. My father's first film where music played an important role was *Bhuvan Shome*. Here, a very talented and highly creative musician, Vijay Raghav Rao, managed to forge a bond with my father just when he was ready to get rid of all conventions and start experimenting. The soundtrack was full of music, and it worked wonderfully with the visual pattern of the film. It was quirky and creative, and my father loved it. The postproduction work was done in Bombay, so I don't know how exactly it came about. That is, I have no idea if my father wanted to impose his idea of using less music and lost, or if it was a conscious decision. One thing is for sure: the collaboration worked. The entire music score was recorded with only five musicians in a small room rather than in a professional studio. The music was also recorded on a quarter-inch tape recorder, which was most unusual, but it saved them money while keeping the production cost low, which was one of my father's major objectives. He worked with Vijay Raghav Rao again, but never created the same magic.

While making *Calcutta 71*, he was looking for a new sound. Perhaps because I used to play Western rock at home, and a fusion album by Ananda Shankar, my father thought of approaching Ananda for his upcoming film. Ananda agreed. They worked together in several of my father's films, and Ananda won a national award for his music in *Chorus*.

As time progressed, my father wanted less and less music in his soundtracks. His later films were more introspective, and he wanted to capture the mood more with silences and incidental sounds. It was not just his music—his dialogues grew sparse too. There would often be long silences between sentences and words. This was often hard for him to communicate to his music directors. I remember many frustrating conversations between them. Not being musically gifted, he could not sing a tune or write music but tried to convey his needs through words, anecdotes, strange verbalizations and rhythms. Some of them got it, but most of them didn't. With each such experience, my father further reduced his inclusion of music.

In *Genesis*, perhaps to satisfy his European production company, my father agreed to work with Ravi Shankar. My father was apprehensive from the start, as he always said that famous composers often start believing that the sole purpose of the film is to showcase their musical genius, and that inevitably creates conflicts. Still, he was excited about the possibility.

The film was edited in Brussels, and they agreed to record the music in Paris. As the film was taking shape, my father fell in love with the recorded sounds from Rajasthan, where the film was shot. In all his other films, they always dubbed the soundtrack as it was very hard to keep the sound recorded during the shoot—there were always too many unwanted sounds. Consequently, not only was the dialogue recorded again in the recording studio but also most of the incidental sounds. Such recreated sounds were never as good and almost never synchronized with the visuals. They were, at best, poor simulacra. However, since that was the norm for everyone, they just learnt to live with it.

For *Genesis*, the international crew was unwilling to accept this option. Also, since the film was mostly shot in remote desert areas, it wasn't too difficult for them to control the unwanted sounds. My father was thrilled to see the results, especially the presence of the small incidental sounds, and he was extremely reluctant to spoil the pristine quality of the soundtrack. I remember a sequence where the visual shows an earthen pot being filled with water. The sound of it, as it was recorded during the shoot, was so perfect and beautiful that there was no way they could have recreated it in post-production. The sound recordist also recorded some local folk music while travelling through that area, and my father liked that too.

Despite explaining all this to Ravi Shankar, he still created a score that would fill most of the soundtrack. After recording the music, the team returned to Brussels to complete the film. During rerecording, my father kept very little of Ravi Shankar's music for the final film.

Next year, after the film was screened at Cannes, it was released in Paris. Ravi Shankar was in the city, and went to watch the film with a couple of his famous musician friends. A day later, he called my father in Calcutta, furious. He told my father that he felt he had been slapped with a sandal in front of his friends—for most of his compositions were gone. My father apologized. I don't think they ever spoke after that.

In 2020, there was an exhibition of Ravi Shankar memorabilia in Chicago. There, among other things, was the jacket of the LP album of *Genesis*. Of course, the commercial recording included more than what was in the actual film. Nisha and I met Ravi Shankar's wife, Sukanya, for the first time, at the inauguration. She is a wonderful person, pleasant and generous. We talked about the album and many common connections, but I could not bring up the incident of the Paris screening. Perhaps she knew about it but was nice enough to make no mention of it.

In *Antareen*, he asked his young cameraman, Sashi Anand, to also compose the music. I was in Chicago then, so I am not sure what made him do that. I also don't know whether Sashi had any musical training. My guess is, Bondhu felt more comfortable conveying the mood he was trying to capture—and more effectively—to Sashi, a nonprofessional already deeply familiar with the film. Looking at the finished film, it is evident that he wanted very sparse music, that too in order to enhance the oppressive loneliness of the film.

The other music director he used more than once was his friend from his formative years—Salil Chowdhury. They started their journey with similar political ideals. Chowdhury was one of the most prominent voices of the organizing songs that activists would sing across the country. Even today, any left-leaning event, especially in West Bengal, cannot happen without a few songs composed by him. However, when he moved to Bombay in the fifties and sixties, his success in commercial cinema started to change his political persona. He remained just as creative, but his focus was on popular music and film songs in Bengali and Hindi. This shift and the physical separation between Calcutta and Bombay created a distance between him and my father. He still came to our house from time to time whenever he visited Calcutta, but the gap was palpable. During some of his visits, we would borrow a harmonium from some neighbours, and sing their IPTA songs. Sometimes Montu-babu, an old singer friend of theirs, would join in. Those were magical moments as the music transported two old friends to their youthful days.

After a long gap, my father collaborated with Salil-kaka on *Akaler Shandhaney*. The film opens with an old organizing song by Salil-kaka; we watch a bus full of the film crew singing as they travel towards their location, to make a film on the Bengal Famine. Leading this song is Montu-babu, who had sung the same song when they all believed a revolution was in the making.

MY FRIENDS, HIS COLLEAGUES

As I reached my teenage years, the relationship between Bondhu and my friends started to slowly transform. I could see that he was forming a direct friendship with some of them without me as an intermediary. He hated being called 'uncle', which is customary in our culture; he insisted my friends call him Mrinal-da, which is how almost everyone else called him. For those unfamiliar with the Bengali cultural conventions, that is how you would address an older brother. Certainly not a friend's father.

When I moved from high school to college, the border between my friend circle and my father's grew blurred. Many remained my friend, while many others crossed over. Among those who were closer to him, many eventually worked with him in some capacity and thus became his colleagues.

The first to do so was my closest school friend, Abhijit Gupta. We both had an interest in fine arts during our high-school days, but in college, he formalized his commitment by joining the Government Art College while I moved towards science. Abhi spent a good part of his day at our place and therefore was very close to the film-production process. Right after he joined art school, my father asked him to design the publicity materials for his next film, *Padatik*. I was a bit nervous—Abhi's experience as a professional graphic artist was rather limited at that time. However, the poster that he designed instantly became an iconic image. To this day, I believe it is one of the best examples of great typographic design in the Bengali language. Abhi went on to design quite a few more posters for my father, and remained a close friend of our family. As an artist, I felt he was a little too ahead of his contemporaries. The art scene in Calcutta, and to some extent in India, was very conservative in those days. As is often the case, the art that sold well defined the reputation of the artist, and the buyers in India only wanted to buy what they already knew. There was no shortage of artists who were willing to feed that market. Abhi wanted to do something different, and was one of the first in the country to try pure conceptual art and installations rather than conventional paintings and sculptures. The marketplace was not yet ready for them, yet Abhi was too stubborn to give in. As a result, he was never appropriately valued by the art world in Calcutta. He slowly became isolated, which resulted in some frustration, but it never swayed his conviction as an artist. We tragically lost him when he was just 60 years old to a rare, but generally non-life-threatening, infection.

Nitish Roy was a classmate of Abhi's at Art College, and that is how I met him and then discovered that we had always been neighbours. Nitish lost his parents early and lived with his elder brother and his wife. His existence in his brother's household was not always smooth and comfortable, and we would often hear about his hardships. Nitish went to a local Bengali-medium school, and never learnt to speak English. After graduating from Art College, Nitish made a living by designing exhibition booths for corporate entities. One morning, in the early eighties, when my father decided to make his next film, *Kharij*, he asked me if one of my friends would be interested in designing the sets. He rarely built sets, as most of his films were shot in real locations. However, in this case, the whole film would take place inside an old tenement building, and he needed the flexibility of working in a studio set. He was unhappy with the film-industry set designers as he felt they were too conventional and could not think beyond the clichés of what a typical interior should look like. Since his close friend and usual set designer, Bansi Chandragupta, had died, he was on the lookout for someone who could replace him.

I was instantly cautious, since none of my friends had ever built a set, and I didn't want to be blamed for the disaster if they failed. So I said that only one person had some experience in building structures, and that was Nitish, but whether he could serve the purpose of the film had to be determined by my father. Bondhu was fine with that and immediately called up Nitish and described the set he wanted: the story revolved around a young lower-middle-class couple with a child. A servant boy dies of carbon monoxide poisoning at the start, and the rest of the film takes place over the next couple of days. Bondhu asked him to come over and discuss it further.

After a couple of hours, Nitish arrived. As they sat down, Nitish's first question was whether the couple had an arranged marriage or a 'love' marriage. My father was surprised and a little annoyed by the question, and asked Nitish why that mattered at all—by the time the film began, they had been married and even had a child. The question was redundant and inconsequential.

Nitish meekly said that if it was an arranged marriage, then they should have got a dowry, which meant the furniture would have been bought at one go and would be of similar design. However, in the case of a love-marriage, the family was unlikely to pay a dowry, and therefore the furniture would have been put together from different sources, maybe even bought second-hand, and the pieces would not match each other.

My father grabbed Nitish's hand and instantly offered him the job.

The set was constructed in a more-or-less unused studio in the north of the city. Aurora Studio had had its glory days but now remained mostly abandoned for the film productions had moved to the south. This gave Nitish the opportunity to take much more time than usual to build the set. Even though it was his first set construction, everyone was truly impressed by the natural and lived-in look he created.

Something unexpected and wonderful happened next. While the film was being shot, Calcutta was hosting its annual film festival. This attracted many serious filmmakers from across India and abroad. When they heard that my father was shooting in the city, many of them wanted to visit the sets and watch him work. This gave Nitish an unexpected exposure. Immediately after returning from Calcutta, Shyam Benegal called my father and asked if Nitish would be interested in working with him. He agreed, and soon became a sought-after art director in the Bombay film industry. He was awarded the national award for art direction three times, beginning with *Kharij*. This is a great example of how luck and serendipity, along with talent, are sometimes needed to achieve fame and fortune.

After Nitish moved to Bombay, my father was on the lookout for a replacement. Another friend of mine, Gautam Bose, whom I came to know through Abhijit and Nitish, filled that role. Gautam was also a student at Art College, but a few years senior to Abhi. He was an excellent draughtsman and worked with both Abhi and Nitish after their graduation. Gautam worked on several of my father's films and eventually became one of the more well-known art directors in the Calcutta film industry.

One of my college-era friends was Sambit Bose. He was a student of commerce at St Xavier's College, with little interest in the subject. After graduation, he was at a loss for he had no interest in pursuing a profession in business. Perhaps since he spent considerable time at our place, he may have developed an interest in films and suddenly decided to apply to FTII. To his surprise, he was accepted. At Pune, there was a rapid transformation in his personality. Each time he visited Calcutta, he seemed more independent, confident and significantly more rebellious.

Sambit's visits were becoming a little stressful for me as he would always contradict my father about some film-related issue and then they'd proceed to have heated arguments. I tried to move the conversations away from such topics, but Sambit would come prepared for a fight, and refuse to budge. However, after his graduation, he returned to Calcutta and started working with my father. At first, he assisted Mahajan-kaka, and later became my father's cinematographer for a few of his films. It was interesting to see that my father fully understood that his initial rebellion was nothing more than a young person finding his voice. Even though my father seemed annoyed by Sambit's constant attacks, none of that played any role when the time came to add Sambit to the team. When Sambit suddenly died in his mid-thirties, my parents were in Brussels, editing *Genesis*. My mother later told me that Bondhu hardly spoke for the next few days.

Another friend of mine from my school and college days was Rahul Bose. He was also the son of one of my father's friends. Rahul was a bully at school, and I was mortally afraid of him. After I moved from South Point to Patha Bhavan in Class 5, I lost touch with him and was quite happy about it. In college, some of my closest friends were from Rahul's class, and we became friends again. However, while we were still doing our undergraduate, Rahul decided to drop out and join the merchant navy. He was mostly at sea, occasionally visiting the city during his breaks. His sea-faring days gave him time to read and think, as there was time every day when he did not have to work. With each visit, we could see a transformation in him towards greater maturity and depth. Finally, one day, when the romanticism of being a sailor was gone, he could no longer tolerate the superficial life aboard a merchant ship, fought with the captain and got himself kicked off of the ship. That was the end of his life as a sailor, and Rahul returned to Calcutta as an intellectual in search of a meaningful profession.

I no longer recall how it happened, but Rahul became one of my father's film assistants and assisted him in several of his later films. My father loved this, as most of his assistants in the past, who were all very competent, did not have the intellectual pre-paredness that Rahul had. Rahul was also part of a documentary crew that made a wonderful and introspective film on my father. He once shared the idea of a film with me regarding the political involvement and idealism that motivated his father and mine, but I don't think he ever got a chance to make it. Rahul eventually left the film industry and devoted his time to founding and running an organization that taught young tribal children in a village near Santiniketan. He is still doing the same.

I often wondered what it felt like to transition from being a friend of mine to becoming a friend and a colleague of my father. Did it create an awkward gap? Did his other team members treat my friends any differently? If there was such a difference, they never expressed it to me, and neither did I sense anything unusual. I just remember that they all maintained a strict barrier between the two roles. When we met as friends, they rarely brought up their pro-fessional world, and I am sure they avoided any explicit mention of our friendship during their film work. It so happened that none of my friends eventually became film directors, except for Nitish, who directed a few inconsequential films. I would have liked to see a film director among my friends.

PART 3
Father

THE STORY COLLECTOR

Bondhu was always in search of stories. In his personal life, he had an acute sense of picking up interesting anecdotes, which he would store in his network of memories to be retrieved at any time the anecdote could fit into a conversation. There was hardly any topic on which he did not have an interesting anecdote to add. These made his conversations interesting and attractive, and they would often turn into a monologue as he would string them together, one contextually following another, into a long discourse. Dipu Bose, a friend of mine, once described them as 'Mrinal-da'r galpomala' or Mrinal-da's necklace of stories.

People who knew him well also knew most of his anecdotes, but since he could string them together in infinite varieties, depending on the context, they never lost their charm. I, for one, knew them all, having listened to them a thousand times, but I still enjoyed them. He also enjoyed telling them, and never wanted to be away from an audience.

Some of those stories included me. He incorporated them into his essays and interviews, and in a few cases, even into his films. Some of them are from my childhood—I don't have any memory of them except for what I heard from my father. However, some others were from my adult life, and I have clear memories of those.

In many cases, when I read his memory of the incident, it was subtly different from mine. The main story would be the same, but the details would change. This bothered me since he was imposing things that were not entirely true, yet people reading them would assume that is what I had said or written in a letter.

Right after we came to Chicago, Ray's *Aparajito* was screened by the University of Chicago's film club. A group of my Bengali friends and I went to watch it. That is a film that always touches me deeply, but then I was freshly away from my mother—and there was a guilt around that. And so the mother-son relationship in the film was pretty close to home; I could not excuse Apu for his insensitivity and selfishness. After the screening, everyone came over to our place, and an interesting argument ensued. Those of my friends who had made up their minds to stay in America felt that the mother was selfish, that she was psychologically blackmailing her son and preventing him from realizing his dreams. I, on the other hand, was far more sympathetic towards the mother and said that I could not blame her for her actions. The next morning, I wrote a letter to my mother about this incident, and promised her that I would return as soon as my studies were over.

Bondhu used that letter not only in an article but also as the basis of a short TV film called 'Aparajit' in his *Kabhi Door Kabhi Paas* series (1985–86). I cannot fault him for fictionalizing some of the details in the film because, after all, it is a fictional work. However, I was upset that the letter he quoted in the article where he said it was written by me was not exactly in my language. The essential facts were the same, but the language was not, nor was the tone I had used. When I communicated my concern to him, he was rather surprised. It was not because he remembered it differently but because he thought what he'd written was better than the original. While I didn't agree that it was necessarily so, my point was that he did not have the right to change anything if he was quoting a real person. That is something he simply could not understand because, according to him, his version made for a better story. After a while, I gave up; I realized that, in his worldview, everything was a story to be used to communicate something. It did not matter to him if a little distortion was needed to make it a better communication tool. To him, the only purpose the real world served was to generate stories that could be harvested, processed and propagated.

Incidentally, some time in the mid-eighties when my father was making *Kabhi Door Kabhi Paas*, Nisha and I were visiting Calcutta. The evening we were to leave for Chicago—always a very painful occasion—all of us were in a rather dark mood. That evening was also when another weekly episode of the series was to be broadcast. The episode was 'Aparajit'. At the end of that short film, the elderly parents arrive at the realization that their only son is not likely to come back, ever. We all watched it together. The film acquired a different emotional strength for the four of us, and that departure from the city was the grimmest I had ever experienced.

In December 1999, I started working for Encyclopædia Britannica. It was a very meaningful job for me, and I was grateful for the opportunity. But it caused me not to keep a promise I made many decades ago when a group of my friends and I had decided that, no matter where we were, we would all gather at the Victoria Memorial in Calcutta on the eve of the millennial new year. That specific spot was selected because we were not sure what Calcutta would look like in thirty years. Perhaps there would be a space-port somewhere, but Victoria Memorial would, no doubt, still be there. Being new at my job, I simply could not take a long holiday right then and had to make that very tough decision of not going back home. It was particularly tough, since it convinced me that I had started to put my career over my personal commitments, and that is exactly what we thought we would never do.

I told my parents about this during a phone call. On the afternoon of 31 December, our phone rang. It was a call from Calcutta, where it was already past midnight. My friends were calling after they'd all met at the designated location, as we had promised. And they told me that even though I could not make it, my father had shown up, representing me. I was deeply touched, and so were my friends.

Bondhu wrote about this incident in an article, and again there were details he made up. As usual, I complained but failed to convince him that he had no right to distort a real incident. His persistent defence was that his version was a better story.

I often wonder how much he manipulated all the other anecdotes with which we are all so familiar. The versions he told became his memory, and he could never remember them any differently or if they were different at all.

In *Matira Manisha*, the younger brother witnesses an aeroplane flying over his village for the first time. That night he has a dream: he is sitting on the back of the mythical bird Garuda and flying across the sky. Bondhu used to say that it was his own childhood experience, when he saw an aeroplane flying over Faridpur for the first time, and that night he dreamt of flying, of seeing see his town, with all the familiar landmarks, from high up. This intrigued me because I wondered whether a child, who has only seen the world from the flat landscape of a delta and never had any access to any tall structure, could imagine what the world would look like from high up. Is an aerial view imaginable for someone with no such experience? Could our mental apparatus allow us to make that imaginary leap and visualize a perspective we had no exposure to in real life or through pictures? I wanted to understand it better. I questioned him in many ways to get a deeper understanding, but the memory he had was as he said it; if it was otherwise, he couldn't retrieve it. Memories are incredibly unreliable things.

Our life trajectory, experience, taste and beliefs distort them in subtle ways, and the story we remember is always the narrative that makes sense.

Bondhu had an intimate relationship with literature. In his pre-filmmaking days, he used to be a voracious reader, spending entire days at the National Library. I am not sure what his motivation was then, but later, his main intention for reading fiction was to seek ideas for his films. His preference was for short stories and novellas with a narrow stage rather than broad novels that covered many characters and a longer time span. For example, one of his favourite novels was Manik Bandyopadhyay's *Padma Nadi-r Majhi*, but he never wanted to make a film about it because of its broad canvas. He did not believe he could do justice to its complexity in a two-hour-long film. He could imagine making a film out of a small segment of the novel, but not the whole thing.

He almost never followed a story completely but used it as a take-off point. He would use the central idea and the storyline and then adapt them to his needs. This caused problems with some well-known writers who would be upset with his deviations. However, these were exceptions to the rule. Most writers understood the need for another creative person to make changes and did not mind. But that is why he never made a film on a story by Rabindranath Tagore, other than the children's short film he made, *Ichchhapuran* (1970). He knew he would have to make many changes, and Visva-Bharati, the caretaker organization of all of Tagore's work, would create a lot of problems. He didn't believe he would get the same freedom that Ray could get because of his and his family's close ties with the institution.

It was not just stories; he also looked at everything in the real world as material for his cinema. He hated touch-tone phones because they robbed him of the visual tension of a rotary dial phone when used by a desperate person. He felt that a closeup of a hand dialling a rotary phone visually captures the caller's tension; there is no such emotional impact in the image of a person pressing buttons. One can find the imagery of a character dialling a rotary dial in a tight closeup in many of his films when rotary phones were the norm, but never after.

As I have mentioned before, he was disappointed when the word for 'no' did not have the same aural punch in Telugu. He did not like a panoramic view of the city showing any trees because a jungle of buildings, with no greenery to interrupt, was his image of a city.

I am digressing, but I remember a conversation between him and Mohit Chattopadhyay about the physicality of media like film or theatre. In literature, one can easily say that a character got agitated and rushed out of the room, toppling over a chair. But in cinema or in theatre, the physical act of a chair toppling comes with the risk of making the moment hilarious. That is, in literature, one has the advantage of only focusing on parts of the physical world, but in cinema, it comes in its entirety, and one must be careful that the parts do not distract the audience.

Long before he made films, his perceptive world revolved around visuals. He used to mention that the Bengali word 'koutuk' (joke/jest) made him think of a raised arm and someone tickling the armpit. Similarly, the word 'bhayankar' (fearsome), with the missing upper bar in the middle in its Bengali form, reminded him of the Howrah Bridge under construction, when the two ends were already built but the middle was still open.

As I was collecting my own stories to write this book, I was fully aware of the fragility and malleability of memories. Through the process of narrating, the stories become real, and objective reality fades away. Such distortions are entirely unintentional in my case; unlike Bondhu, I do not believe in the primacy of stories. I think the stories that remain closest to reality are also the most interesting.

TO THOSE WHO KNEW HIM

So, what kind of a human being was he? Different people obviously saw different aspects of his personality. None of us share our entire self with every person we meet. However, I had the opportunity to see him interact with a wide variety of people, so let me try to form a composite picture of his most essential traits.

The first attribute apparent to most people who knew him intimately was his sense of humour. He could see the funny side of most situations and was eager to share it with others. The main source of most of his humour was his tolerance, or even fascination, for self-ridicule. Most of the funny stories he shared were about himself as an awkward, underconfident, bumbling man. There was a whole range of such anecdotes, many of which I have already shared. They date back to his days in Faridpur, his student days in Calcutta, his early professional days. However, interestingly, these stories became less frequent as he became more of a celebrity. Is that because he was also convincing himself to be beyond such frailties, or is it that we can have a more objective view of the distant past while the recent past remains more subjective?

He most enjoyed it when my mother told stories about him in which he appeared pathetic and ridiculous. My mother had a great collection of such anecdotes, and being an actor, she could tell them with great effect. Bondhu would listen to them with a shy smile and a twinkle in his eyes. He never intervened in her storytelling, only sometimes reminded her to tell another related one in case she missed it. I think his greater joy was to watch my mother perform and the effect she had on an audience. I wish someone had recorded these stories as my mother told them, but that was long before the ubiquitous cameras in everyone's hands.

My father's sense of humour was not always benign. He could sometimes say things that may be funny to most but also cause great embarrassment to others. My mother and I would try to defuse such situations or scold him for doing so. He never protested at our corrections, but we had little effect on his future behaviour. The only situation that he realized was a mistake was if he'd made a funny comment about one of his subordinates. We would point out that he had taken advantage of his superior rank; the person made fun of could not reciprocate with a similar joke directed at my father. The next day he would try to salvage the situation by being extra friendly towards that person.

The other attribute visible to everyone who knew him was his intense anger. His outbursts were well known to his team and occurred in the tense atmosphere of the production process, especially during their shoots. He could be intensely caustic and ruthless at anyone who made a mistake from his point of view. Everyone on his team knew not to fight back, to simply absorb the reprimand. As far as I can tell, no one held a grudge against him for these outbursts. This was mainly because he would forget about it all by that evening, and be back to his friendly self.

However, his anger towards people outside his team, usually because of their political views or criticism of his work, was intense and persistent. He never practised any tact towards such people, and publicly expressed his feelings even when he knew the effect would go against his best interests. He made an incredible number of enemies, and that certainly made his life difficult and his successes attenuated. He knew it, but was unapologetic and reckless. For example, during the last decade of his life, he was bitterly critical of the local state government and its leader. This resulted in him being eliminated from all government-sponsored events, awards and discussions, yet it had no impact on his continued public bitterness towards the administration.

Bondhu had always carried an inflated sense of self-confidence. I am not sure where it came from, but even before he was successful or received any degree of public acclaim, he was convinced he was special. He interacted with everyone from this self-imagined elevated state. There was, however, never any pompousness to it, and therefore it did not come across as ridiculous or offensive. It simply conveyed the sense that he was to be taken seriously. I remember, whenever he called any official service, such as the phone company or a government department, he would start it with: 'This is Mrinal Sen', followed by a short pause for the information to sink in before continuing with the rest of his complaint or request. This made sense once he became famous, but he did so even before anyone knew who he was.

This was also very apparent in the way he interacted with the biggest names in world cinema, even before his stature was fully established. He naturally treated them as equals, never showing any hint of inferiority or servility, and not surprisingly, that changed their attitude as well. Instead of seeing him as a newcomer from the third world, they immediately responded with respect and treated him as a member of their fraternity. Any time he sensed a slight discrepancy in how a major film festival was treating him compared with some of the world's best, especially from Europe or America, he would point it out and make sure they rectified their preferential treatment. Even at home, long before he made a name for himself, his relationship with Ray was not one of reverence but that of equals. This became particularly apparent when Ray wrote a letter to the editor of the *Statesman* after they published a positive review of *Akash Kusum*. This started a months-long war of words between the two. Ray was already considered a world master while my father was a newcomer, trying to establish himself. I am not sure where he got the confidence to pick a fight with Ray, but he did, and perhaps that changed the equation of their mutual respect.

When my father was just starting to get recognition in the West, the Venice Film Festival picked *Bhuvan Shome* as part of their official selection. This was a major break for him, and understandably, he was very happy. When the ticket arrived for his travel, it was an Economy Class one. He knew only too well that the same festival would not dare to send such a ticket to a well-known film personality from Europe or America. He immediately wrote back: he would attend only if he was sent a First Class ticket. It was a huge risk, as it could have annoyed the festival officials and affected his future relationships in the industry. He failed to see any of that. Interestingly, the festival wrote back that the Economy Class ticket had been a clerical mistake; here was a First Class ticket for him.

One of the traits I could feel most acutely was my father's surprising sense of psychological perception. He could see through people and situations with astonishing accuracy and confidence. Like any son, there were plenty of reasons and occasions when I wanted to hide something from him. Yet I failed almost every time due to his penetrating insight. Be it a faint infatuation with a girl, a slight conflict with a friend, a hint of trouble at work—he always knew something was afoot. Whatever brain quality gives us the ability to peer into another person's mind—what is known in cognitive science as the Theory of the Mind—he had an abundance of it. This also helped him communicate with his actors.

Perhaps the most negative aspect of his character was his self-centred perspective. It was not the trait of a selfish person who only cares about their personal well-being and creature comforts. But in his creative life, he only cared about what was important to him. However, I cannot single him out in this respect. Because of my father, I was fortunate to have watched, from close quarters, many people with exceptional talents and accomplishments; every one of them shared this trait. Of course, simply being self-centred does not guarantee success. However, even with all the other talents and qualities, one may also have to be selfish to make one's mark.

The person who had to pay the most for this was my mother. It started with the poverty she had to endure during the first half of her married life. At times, even survival was tough, yet my father would not budge from his determination to make the kind of films he believed in. Of course, looking back, after his success, one can easily glorify such dedication to one's conviction—but what if he failed and was discarded by history? The only thing that would have remained true would have been my mother's suffering. History is not so kind to people who indulge their idiosyncrasies at the cost of the people around them, but success changes the lens through which we judge them.

After *Bhuvan Shome*, his financial crisis started to ease a little but was not completely gone. I remember, in the early seventies, he borrowed ten thousand rupees from a film-industry money lender. They were called handi-wala, but I am not sure where the term came from. They gave loans without collaterals, based on the borrower's recognizability. However, the interests were exorbitant. We had to pay 5 per cent of the principal every month, which came to five hundred rupees. The lender was not interested in getting the principal, but was insistent on getting his interest at the beginning of each month. I dreaded his phone calls, as he was rough and almost insulting even if we were late by a few days. It was my job to deliver an envelope with the five hundred rupees at the start of each month to the medical-supply store from where he ran his business. This went on for years, but we could not pay back the principal.

Even after our financial problems eased a little, my father's self-absorbed lifestyle affected the people around him. He travelled extensively during the seventies and eighties, mostly to international film festivals. He made a point that the festival committees also invite my mother, which was the norm with other film personalities. Therefore, my mother visited hundreds of cities in the world with him. Of course, it was only but natural that she want to do some sightseeing. But she always regretted that she never saw anything beyond the hotel lobby and the movie theatres, since my father was not interested in anything but watching films and talking to people.

At home, he had visitors from early morning till late at night; he also used our home as his production office. Since we always lived in a small flat, this caused a lot of stress for my mother. The drawing room was always full of visitors, with constant demands for rounds of tea. When he needed to talk to a few people in private, he would bring them into the bedroom. I did the same with my friends. My mother never had her own space where she could relax until we moved to Beltala Road.

When Nisha and I moved to Chicago, I often asked them to visit us. My mother was always eager, but we could rarely convince my father. His excuse was always his work, even when he was between projects and wasn't all that busy. The few times he came, it was always because he had been invited by the Chicago International Film Festival and my mother forbade him from turning them down. There was only the one time when they came only for us—when Nisha was recovering from her major brain surgery and was in no shape to travel. I used that occasion to coerce my father to come over, despite his excuses of work. I think the reason he did not want to come was the boredom he felt here. On most of his visits, we had to go to work, at least for some of the time. So he had nothing to do and no one to talk to during the day. I recall coming back early from work one afternoon, and not finding my father in our apartment. I finally found him sitting on the floor behind our dining table, intently leafing through our thick telephone directory. I asked him what he was looking for, and he replied that he was looking for common Bengali last names. I realized how bored he was and felt a bit sorry for him.

His self-centredness may suggest that he lacked empathy, but that was certainly not the case. If anything, I believe his strong sense of empathy was the motivating factor behind most of his actions. His preoccupation with poverty and lower-middle-class existence was not only a cerebral concern, it was also a deeply felt emotion.

Before Nisha and I got married, Nisha was working on her Master's thesis on protein-calorie malnutrition. So she often had to visit a local children's hospital where most of the patients were from extremely poor backgrounds, suffering from acute malnutrition. One day, she asked me to take some pictures of those children for use in her thesis. My first day of photography failed to yield any results due to a camera malfunction. So I borrowed a camera from Sandip Ray and went back after three days. By then, two of the children I'd seen just a few days ago had died. The living were also on the brink of dying. When I shared these stories with my father, he was visibly shaken and wanted to see for himself. He wanted to make a film about this, and went back to the hospital with his movie camera. The film was never made, but I knew that impulsive reaction had been genuine.

My father had an interesting relationship with Nisha. He knew her at first as one more high-school friend, but much later, when we became a couple, he took more interest in her. What immediately attracted him to her was that she was not a Bengali. Whenever he announced our developing relationship to his friends, the first thing he would mention was that she was a Gujarati. My choice must have reflected his constant desire to break from the norm. In his youth, against the backdrop of the Hindu–Muslim riots in our state, he wanted to marry a Muslim woman. He did not have anyone in mind—he simply liked the idea. However, that desire fizzled away when he met my mother. He carried strong feelings against all types of Bengali chauvinism, and Nisha's non-Bengali status was a source of great pride.

I cannot say for sure that was also not an important a factor for me. As a young man, every time I met someone, I had to sort out how much of that person's interest in me was influenced by my father's reputation. This problem is unique to people with celebrity parents, but is very real. Nisha came from a very different cultural milieu, and even though she was aware of Bondhu's identity, she was not as impressed as someone from a Bengali intellectual background would have been. That was reassuring for me.

The relationship between Nisha and Bondhu remained somewhat aloof until we got married. On one occasion, while we were still dating, he wanted Nisha to play a nurse in *Ek Din Pratidin*. She was supposed to walk down a hospital corridor and announce to a group of waiting relatives that a certain patient had died. I was terrified by the idea, since I knew he was prone to lose his temper during his shoots, and I did not want Nisha to face his wrath. My mother was also tense, and decided to attend the shoot, just in case she needed to ease any awkwardness. Nisha was making horrible technical mistakes, and each time, instead of being apologetic, she kept laughing at her own mistakes. That made my mother and me even more nervous, and we were waiting for my father to explode. But, to everyone's surprise, he maintained a pleasant demeanour.

His inner state of mind became apparent, however, when he screamed at another elderly actor for a minor mistake.

Right after we got married, Nisha told us one morning that she wanted to keep using her maiden name. While that is far more common these days, it was not so in our social set in those days. That one act of openly asserting her identity changed the relationship between Nisha and my father. Since then, I could always see in him a deeper sense of respect towards her. Nisha also told my mother that she did not want to wear sindoor on her forehead, the vermillion that was a sign of a married woman. My mother may not have been all that happy, as she always worried more about our relatives, but she accepted Nisha's decision. Any time we attended a family event, Bondhu made sure there was no implicit pressure on her to conform and lashed out at any relative if they made the mistake of asking Nisha why the new bride was not wearing sindoor.

However, there were times when he did try to interfere and we came dangerously close to conflict. One evening during the first month of our marriage, we were all getting ready to attend some cultural event involving my father. Nisha got dressed in a sari and came out of her room. Bondhu did not like the sari, but instead of telling her directly, he tried to be tactful and asked her a couple of times if she thought it looked good on her. Nisha got the rather broad hint, took it in good humour and changed into a more traditional silk sari. If they did not have the relationship they had, this could have turned into an unfortunate situation.

Every time he went abroad, he would bring back small gifts for my mother and Nisha, usually two identical pieces of some kind of local jewellery. When Nisha pointed out that it would be better to bring two different kinds, as they could share them, he responded that it was a conscious decision on his part—he did not want the difference to be the source of any rift between Nisha and my mother.

He became even more protective of Nisha after I left for Chicago and she remained in Calcutta to complete her PhD. One day, somehow, a small ant got into her eye and could not be dislodged. It was very painful. My father took charge, something he seldom did, and rushed her to an eye doctor. This became a story he would tell anyone who cared to listen. He felt a great pride in playing father to Nisha.

Soon after we moved to Chicago, Nisha's father suddenly died. Nisha was profoundly upset and asked Bondhu to step up as a father. He visited Nisha's mother at least once a month to check on her. This was very uncharacteristic of him and my mother, who barely left home to visit relatives and friends. As my father's health deteriorated, Nisha ended up spending more time with him, and visited Calcutta couple of times a year when I could not. He was appreciative of her visits and very comfortable when Nisha took care of his little needs in my absence.

My father was a complex individual who wanted to live an honest life on his own terms. If I must imagine the most enviable aspect of his life, it would be that he somehow managed to live his life exactly how he wanted, and never compromised. Few people get to say that. Despite that, he had many regrets. He was acutely aware of his mediocrity, and desperately wanted to live life over again. The next time, he would make fewer mistakes.

AS A FATHER

As I was growing up, Bondhu did not play the traditional role of a father. I don't remember him as the rock-solid superhuman who could protect and guide me. On the contrary, I found him a slightly eccentric, somewhat unreliable, irresponsible and bumbling adult. For all the fatherly qualities, I looked up to my uncle, Anu. There were moments of friendship between my father and me, but it was more as between equals than as between parent and child.

Once, playing in the neighbourhood park aged ten or eleven, I fell. My chin hit a concrete step, resulting in a wide gash that bled profusely. The older kids took me to the local pharmacy, and had the wound stitched up. When I was brought home, my mother was very alarmed about it all, and I felt like a bit of a hero. That was my first major accident, and a big deal for my mother and me.

My father was out of town and supposed to come back late in the evening. I was anticipating the drama of him walking in, seeing my prominent bandage, then hearing my story with awe and shock. I had been at the centre of attention that whole evening, and I wanted it to continue. As expected, my father finally arrived. As he came into the bedroom, my mother blurted out that I had a bad fall and needed a few stitches. He had a fleeting expression of concern; he touched my forehead for temperature even though a fever

155

was not my problem, and then, with his hand still on my forehead, started telling my mother about the exciting events of his trip.

I was devastated.

A few years after their marriage—when my mother still had romantic feelings about their relationship—on the morning of their wedding anniversary, she asked my father to bring home some flowers. Perhaps she tried to jog his memory, but there was no reaction. Ma was understandably upset all day. In the evening, when my father returned home, his hands were empty. This was more than what she could tolerate. My mother reminded him in a stern voice. He immediately said that he had not forgotten, dipped his hand into his kurta pocket, fished out a small sal-leaf package and handed it over to her with the proud smile of a person who can remember his instructions. It was a package of low-cost flower petals sold in the market for Hindu religious rituals.

This unflattering image I had of my father continued for a while until I was a teenager and my own interests began to undergo a transition. Because of the unusual school I attended, where most of the teachers were formidable intellectuals with a wide range of interests, I started discovering a world outside that of games and sports. I began to read other kinds of books, to appreciate more grown-up music, to attend art exhibitions. With my horizons expanding rapidly, I quickly lost interest in my friends and started finding the conversations in our living room far more interesting. I would sit in a corner, pretending to study, but actually listening to what was being discussed. This was an incredibly exciting phase for me when an entirely different world was slowly opening its wings, and I wanted to belong in it. In this new world, there was a different way to measure one's worth, and I quickly realized that my father had something in him that most people around him found extremely valuable. That they looked up to him.

It took a long fourteen years to develop, but suddenly he became my hero. He remained unreliable and undependable. Despite that, I started to respect him for his intellectual prowess. Most interestingly, those negative qualities that I did not care for earlier suddenly became idiosyncratic ornamentations of his total package, and even though they were not to be admired, they became something endearing and likable. Finally, I could feel proud of him. With this pride also came the sadness that he was not getting his due respect. I wanted him to succeed, I wanted him to win his arguments, I desperately wanted to understand everything he talked about. I did not have to wait too long. Within a year of my newfound entry into this world of ideas, he made *Bhuvan Shome* and finally attained that special place that I thought he deserved.

Simultaneously, my father also started taking pride in my new identity. Within a few years, I could see that he intently listened to what I thought about things. By the time I was done with high school, he had started to treat me as a grown-up. We fought, we argued, we shared our thoughts. During all this, I don't recall a single moment where he tried to mould me or push me in a certain direction. I could see that I was appreciated more when I disagreed and showed signs of original thinking, whether my arguments were right or wrong. These encouragements must have convinced me to become more of a contrarian than a believer. I became the strongest critical voice in our household, and he appreciated that.

After the first screening of his latest film, after the random discussions in front of the theatre, after longer discussions with friends who came home with him were gone, after a few lengthy phone calls with viewers, we would settle down for our dinner, late at night. That is when he would ask me what I thought. If I started with a thumbs up, I would see a sense of deep relief on his face. There would be a genuine smile of accomplishment that few people could witness.

With some regret, I must admit that rarely happened. I would most often start with my reservations. That was not because I was cruel, but because I wanted his films to be as flawless as possible, and I wanted everyone that mattered to like his films. I was watching them not just from my point of view but also from the perspective of everyone I cared about. This combined perspective was necessarily more critical than my singular opinion, and that's what came out during those dinner conversations. He would listen to them with utmost seriousness, sometimes object, but mostly remain silent and deep in thought. If I continued for too long, then at some point he would ask if I had liked anything at all. And that would make me realize my cruelty, and I would start to mention what had appealed to me. My mother listened to it all, sometimes agreeing with me, sometimes not. She was more interested in knowing what other people had to say and asked my father specifically about every person's reaction. Looking back, I realize I should have been more tactful and sensitive. My youthful pride and confidence got the better of me. Now I know that sometimes support is more important than honest rationality.

Things got harder when I moved to Chicago. No longer connected with the filmmaking process, I could not provide ongoing feedback. He would always send me his script and I would send back my comments though I knew that the film would deviate significantly. When the film was complete, he would send me a VHS tape. This usually came in the mail, which took weeks. Then Nisha and I—and later, her sister Jagriti—would watch the finished product on a television screen. The magic of watching it in a dark room, on a big screen, with an audience full of friends, was gone. It was a clinical viewing where emotions were constrained and cold criticality prevailed. There was a gloomy sense of premonition: What if I didn't like it, how would I tell Bondhu? I was more careful by then, and perhaps a little more detached.

Unlike earlier, I would always start with what I liked followed by what I didn't. I could no longer see the reactions on his face, and the conversation on the phone or email exchanges were more distant in so many ways.

Like any father, he wanted me to succeed. Yet my career trajectory was less than spectacular. My PhD took a lot longer than usual as I squandered my time on other things, including a part-time job I did at a lab that I truly enjoyed. As a result, it was getting frustrating for me, and I often thought of quitting my PhD program. The only thing that stopped me was my father's disappointment. I was afraid of his reaction, and stayed on course.

When I finally received my degree, he, for the first time, explicitly asked me to return. He spoke with people in India, and they suggested potential job opportunities. However, none of them seemed exciting; I wanted to continue at my lab but now as a full-time employee. I enjoyed my titles, both of Scientist and of Vice President of Technology at a small start-up that the lab's work spawned. I also enjoyed a decent salary that finally allowed us to enjoy the aspects of this country that we could not afford as students. By then, Nisha had also finished her second Master's degree in education and started teaching at the prestigious Laboratory Schools at the University of Chicago.

Even though we were certain we would eventually return to India, my father could see the writing on the wall—that we may never come back for good. He shared his conviction with my mother, and they both started mentally preparing for an old age where they would be coping alone. We, on the other hand, never applied for our green cards; why go through the hassle when we wouldn't need them, after all? Ultimately, my father's perception proved to be more accurate. We gradually started to accumulate reasons for why staying here made more sense in terms of our own lives. Nisha loved her job. I eventually joined Encyclopædia

Britannica, and there was great joy in being part of an institution that is more than two centuries old. By then, we had more friends here than in Calcutta. After Nisha's father's untimely death, her sister and mother came over. Very soon, we had too many entanglements, and finally, we decided to stay here. Though it did not come as a surprise to my parents, saying so was one of the hardest things we had to do.

Bondhu was proud when he heard that I was working for Britannica. It was a name known to him, and he could proudly announce it to his friends. He would have preferred if I were to become some sort of a celebrity, but this was an acceptable alternative. He always realized that fame was far easier in popular media than science or technology or academics. While talking to some of my academic friends, he almost apologized for this asymmetry. He acknowledged that it was far more difficult to make a name, say, in physics, than making a so-so film that could make someone a recognizable name in popular media.

About ten years after joining Britannica, while visiting Calcutta, a random thought started taking shape in my mind. I always enjoyed painting as a hobby, and I loved computer programming. One of my strongest passions was designing and building electronic circuits, and I loved building mechanical things. So why not put them all together? The thought started percolating in my mind, and when I came back to Chicago, I wanted to give it a try. This was possibly the smartest decision I ever made, because there is one thing I now realize—regret is the worst thing one can live with, far worse than failure.

I have taken many drawing and painting courses since I came to Chicago, but only as a hobby. At the ripe old age of fifty-five, I wanted to embark on a new journey and wanted to take up art-making seriously. Of course, I had no illusions and knew that it would be nearly impossible to break into a highly competitive field at this age, but it did not matter. I just wanted to enjoy the process and enjoy being part of this world. However, when a prestigious local art organization accepted me into their artist-incubation program, I realized I could masquerade as an artist after all. This news made my father very happy. Unfortunately, I have never been able to show him my work. Nisha always wanted me to organize a show in Calcutta while my father was alive, but that never happened. Towards the end, each time I visited Calcutta, he would ask me to show photographs of my work on the computer. He no longer had the attention span to look at a long series of screen images and videos, neither did he have the cognitive strength to comprehend my explanations. But he would still stare at the screen with a big smile.

A SEEDLING IN A FOREST

I have been mostly talking about the people around me. But the story will remain incomplete unless I also include what it was like to grow up surrounded by giants. So let me indulge in mentioning a few things about my own experiences and the trajectory of my life.

As I was growing up, I mostly met people who had a public persona, if they were not outright famous. Ordinary people are only known to others through familial relationships, or through direct or indirect friendships. However, certain people reach a state of celebritydom where complete strangers will know of them through their work. That circle, big or small, makes someone a public figure. In that sense, almost everyone I knew in my childhood was famous. Some were only known in a small circle, some had a widespread aura, some others could be easily recognized in public spaces.

In my household, my uncle Anup Kumar was a very popular Bengali screen and stage actor. Therefore, whenever I was with him at the market, or the zoo, or on the street—he was immediately spotted and often pestered by absolute strangers. If I was in a car with him and the car stopped at a traffic light, invariably there would be people staring at us and even trying to start a conversation. This always put him in a foul mood.

My father was not recognizable initially, but that started to change as I grew up. He would draw a slightly different type of attention than my uncle, and people were not as intrusive. My mother was far less recognizable but was still a public figure.

Growing up in this atmosphere, it seemed more natural for a person to be famous than to be an ordinary human being. So, naturally, the only future I could imagine was that as a famous individual, but in what capacity and at what scale were the primary speculations of my persistent childhood daydreams, though none of these scenarios included an image of me as a filmmaker. My interest swayed towards science and technology during my early teens, and my heroes, my dreams of fame and my fantasies of changing the world revolved around that. While my dreams were intense, and my confidence in achieving this state was certain in my mind, I did little to achieve my goals. In retrospect, could it be that the abundance of famous people in my surroundings created a false sense of ease and inevitability?

The most obvious and almost guaranteed way to gain public attention for me was to follow my father's profession. This is what was expected of me by the outside world, and I am often asked why I did not. The entry would have been relatively easy. I was intimately familiar with the process and the skills involved, and I would have received guidance and help from my father and his crew. Perhaps financiers would also have been willing to take a chance on me, as they could have utilized the natural curiosity of the audience. Therefore, the remaining issue was whether I could have delivered. That is hard to guess; as objectively as I can think of my own capabilities, I probably would not have been a complete failure. As I've said before, it is relatively easier to gain celebrity in mass media, such as cinema, than in academics. Therefore, even if I failed to make any critically acclaimed films, it is reasonable to assume that I could have gained some degree of mass recognizability and fame.

My pride in myself, which my parents nurtured, closed that door for me. It was certainly not a conscious decision, but being a filmmaker was a little too easy and expected, and I drifted in a different direction. Looking back, I was perhaps also in competition with my father, and wanted to carve out a path where his help and influence would be completely absent.

I remember an incident when *Calcutta 71* was released in a single theatre in central Calcutta. That was a politically turbulent time, and for the young leftists, watching the film became a sort of political act. There used to be a long queue every morning to purchase tickets, and people often waited for hours. I had just finished high school and wanted to invite some friends to see the film. So I decided to stand in that line. It was an interesting experience, listening to the conversations around me, both about the film and contemporary politics. Of course, no one knew my connection to the filmmaker. After many hours, when I was finally close to the ticket window, Mukul-babu, the production manager, happened to be walking towards the theatre for some business. He spotted me in the line and was surprised and visibly annoyed that I had decided to wait with the rest rather than ask him to organize a few passes. He grabbed my arm and pulled me away and said he would get me the tickets. I could not turn around and face my fellow ticket seekers.

I went to a most unusual school, where the ideology was against the usual focus on test grades and which cultivated creativity and independent thinking. Unlike many of my classmates, I took this to heart and believed it was utterly unimportant to score well. Therefore, my high-school results were dismal—they were so poor that it was impossible for me to even obtain the application form for local colleges. I was in a crisis and ran from college to college, just to get an admission form while continuously lowering the quality of colleges I was targeting. Finally, I learnt that St Xavier's

College, a prestigious institution, did not care about official grades and made its decisions based on its own admission test. It was a test based on critical thinking, and I did very well. After I gained admission, I learnt from the vice principal that I could have got into this, and almost any other college, by virtue of a national scholarship I had won earlier. I had sat for a scholarship test called National Science Talent Search, and been a winner, ranking nationally at thirtieth place. I wish I had known that earlier, before running about the city with no success. During all this time, my father never tried to use his influence to help me. Nor did it ever occur to me to leverage his connections.

Despite my dreams of becoming a great scientist, I ignored my studies completely and barely scraped through my undergraduate courses. I still enjoyed reading about science outside my curriculum, but did not invest the time and energy that is essential to master a subject. There was no rigour. I had close friends doing spectacularly well in physics, and I could readily see the gap between their deep mastery of the subject and my broad but superficial understanding. That was when I realized I didn't have what it takes to be the next Albert Einstein. So I switched from pure physics to applied physics, a hybrid between physics and engineering. That too failed to capture my imagination, and I finished my postgraduate degree with no sense of accomplishment.

I have always been interested in computers, and learnt how to program a computer even before I had access to one. During my college days, when Calcutta hosted its first book fair, there was a section called Book Bazar where publishers dumped their unsold books at very low prices. This was heaven for me, and among many others, I picked up a book called *Design for a Brain* by W. Ross Ashby. That book had a huge influence on me, and ever since, I have wanted to learn more about computers and the mind. I got the opportunity when I joined the Master's program in computer science at the Indian Statistical Institute, and for the first time, I was truly interested in my studies and did very well.

After graduation, I stayed at the same institute to embark on my PhD. However, when my advisor moved to the US, I decided to do the same and ended up in Chicago. Incidentally, my PhD advisor at the University of Illinois did his PhD under the guidance of the same W. Ross Ashby whose book changed my trajectory. Once again, my old disease of drifting away set in, and I paid more interest to the part-time job in a research lab than to my thesis work at the university. I achieved some degree of success in that work, but it delayed my research. By the time I finally obtained my doctoral degree, I had little enthusiasm to pursue an academic life. That was a huge mistake, but I allowed myself to give up.

I was fortunate that I have been genuinely appreciated and respected in all the things I have done since then in the industry, but I missed pure research. I am often told that my contributions have been creative and intelligent, and every organization I worked for left the door open for me. But these minor successes were far from my childhood dreams.

My father, though he never expressed it, was also disappointed. He wanted me to become accomplished and significantly contribute to whatever discipline I chose. My association with Encyclopædia Britannica made him proud, as it is an institution he recognized and respected. What finally made him truly happy was when he heard that I had started making art as a hobby and gained some limited recognition. However, by then, he was too old to fully comprehend what I was doing.

Now, at sixty-eight, I have a clearer perspective of my capabilities and weaknesses. I no longer dream of fame and fortune. One of the tragedies of age is that even your daydreams are moderated by reality. Dreaming of fantastical futures, which came so easily in my younger days, became impossible as I got older. Every indulgent daydream is interrupted by a part of my brain that reminds me of the unlikeliness of the dream. Fortunately, this oppression of reality was accompanied by an altered understanding of what makes life more meaningful. As I got older, especially during the last ten years, the need to obtain external recognition started to ebb away. I still enjoy appreciation, but I feel more satisfied and fulfilled by my inner richness. Whenever I feel I have a deeper understanding of the world I live in, there is a tremendous inner joy that is hard to explain. I don't think I am intrinsically smarter today than I was in my earlier years, but I can connect various things I have learnt over the years, and this ability to connect dissimilar things is deeply satisfying and triggers a desire to share them with others.

About ten years ago, while talking to a young colleague, I expressed my disappointment at not finding the time to read as much as I used to. In response, he asked me roughly how many books I typically read. I said if I could finish one book a month, I would consider that a good month. He said that was not so bad— one book a month translates to a dozen books a year. I paused for a few seconds, did a quick mental calculation, and realized that at this rate, I have about three hundred books left to read—about one or two bookshelves worth. This was a profound moment of realization of how short life is and that there is no time to waste. The first thing I did was to stop reading 'trashy' books, as I did not want to fill up my list of three hundred with junk. It also made me find more time to read, and since then, I have been averaging about one book a week. Therefore, my realistic book list has expanded from a pathetic three hundred to a slightly more meaningful twelve hundred. Still a very sobering number, which I cannot waste on books that will not make me grow. My personal definition of a good read is one where I will be a slightly different person after I finish it. I have also learnt to constrain my curiosity a little, and started focusing on a few interrelated subjects which in turn allow me to enjoy the deeper satisfaction of knowing a few things in depth rather than having a superficial understanding of many things. Even though I am the same person today, I certainly feel more intelligent now than even ten years ago, and this further enhances my regret that I didn't learn to focus much earlier in life. Broad curiosity is a perfect ingredient for a rich life but is only valued when one is exceptionally good at one thing.

I will probably stop working in a couple of years. I want to use the time between my retirement and when my mind starts to betray me to do things that are meaningful to me. It could be more reading, making art, perhaps writing more. I am not a writer, but I want to improve my skills. It may seem absurd that someone at seventy wants to develop a new skill, but the regret of not even trying would be far more painful. I am glad that such caution did not stop me from starting my art career when I was past fifty, and I will be glad if I am not too cautious about writing. I know full well that one may not become a meaningful artist or a writer by starting this late, but I can at least say that I tried. I wish I could share all this with my father. It would have aligned with how he lived his life—taking risks and defying age.

THE LAST FEW YEARS

My family always dreamt of moving into our own flat. But the price of a flat we would like, located in a part of the city we preferred, was always just beyond our means. Finally, in 2002, my father accumulated some extra money, and Nisha and I could help, and we pooled our resources to purchase our flat on Padmapukur Road. It was larger than our earlier flats—with a bedroom for my parents, one for us, a large dining and living space, and finally, a small office for my father. It was also a brighter place with more natural light and air.

This move also coincided with the end of my father's professional life as a filmmaker. He finished *Amar Bhuvan* exactly as he was about to turn eighty. Something was also changing within him at the same time. I remember the first time we visited them at the new house, I was surprised to see how much he cared about the upkeep of the place. This was the first kitchen where we had installed a 'chimney' over the stove to prevent a greasy layer forming on everything in the house. The manufacturer's representative had explained to my father that the hood needed to be cleaned regularly for it to perform well. I noticed that this had become an obsession with him, and he would badger the woman who cooked for us to clean it regularly. One early morning, I came into the kitchen to make a cup of tea and was surprised to see him trying to clean it himself with a small piece of facial tissue clutched in his inept hands. That was my first realization that something was changing. A person who barely knew what the kitchen looked like was getting domesticated. A part of it was, of course, the pride of ownership, but his interest in the home was more than that.

That same year, Nisha was diagnosed with a brain tumour that had to be removed by a complicated surgery that took more than half a day. After the surgery, one side of her face was paralysed, and even walking was difficult. The doctors did not allow for any travel, and she needed me to take care of her. This caused a pause in our Calcutta trips. I was missing my parents, and insisted they visit us instead. Despite my father's reluctance, my mother and I were able to coerce him into agreeing. During these two weeks, we often had friends visiting us with the primary intent of meeting my parents. On one such evening, Bondhu started to tell a long anecdote to my friends. I knew them all, and remembered how interesting he could make them. But that time I could see my friends getting restless as his stories became repetitive and predictable.

The following fifteen years of his life comprised a slow decline of his cognitive abilities. Sometimes the decline was rapid, followed by a long plateau. First to go was his interest in the external world, especially the world of cinema. He watched fewer films, and since he stopped travelling to international festivals, his exposure also became limited.

The next thing to go was his ability to react to conversations and pull up the right anecdotes. Instead, he would talk about what was already on his mind and force that topic into the conversation. What had been his hallmark—reacting quickly to a subject and connecting it with one of his thousands of stories—was fading away.

Even though his alertness was fading, he could write very well, for that created no pressure on him to react quickly. He wrote two of his books during this period. We started collaborating as partners during the writing of *Always Being Born*, but it took a very long time. He would write a chapter or a portion, and send it to me through email, expecting an answer right away. The problem was the time difference and the fact that I had a full-time job. He would get very impatient if I took more than a few hours to respond and would start sending impatient reminders, telling me how important it is for me to write back. I did my best and sent back my comments as soon as possible. The problem was made worse when he would read through my comments, make a few changes, then send the chapter back again. I could never teach him how to use 'track changes' in Microsoft Word, so I had no way of knowing where the changes were and had to reread the whole thing. Though it imposed a more significant tax on my time, it proved to be better, as each time I was reading it as a complete piece rather than reading the scattered sentences. It took a very long time for the book to take shape, but we were both happy, and my father was especially proud of it. It was published the following year, in 2004.

Unfortunately, the publishers did not have the distribution power to adequately promote the book. When I questioned his choice of a well-meaning but small publisher instead of one of the bigger houses, he answered that they were very nice. That was always his answer to many such decisions—he picked them without considering all the practical elements. The only thing that mattered to him was whether they were good, intelligent people with integrity.

Always Being Born was a completely nonlinear book. Unlike many autobiographies, it did not tell the story of his life chronologically, but the thread that connected things was conceptual. It was structurally very similar to his conversational style. He had a massive bag of interesting anecdotes. He would start with one, then, depending on the context of the conversation, pick another that somehow thematically connected with the first. He could go on and on. The book was similar in structure: each chapter dealt with a particular idea, and he connected many anecdotes, picked from different times in his life, to tell the story and make his point. The book captured him, his perspectives and his times very well.

He worked on several books during the next decade, both in English and Bengali. He went back to his favourite topic, Chaplin, and wrote a very personal book on him. It is interesting to note that one of his first books was also on Chaplin. This was published before he started making films, and the cover was designed by Ray before he began making films. Therefore, in a way, Chaplin formed the opening and closing parentheses for the rest of Bondhu's career. Chaplin was one of my father's few heroes, and the only time he met Chaplin, very briefly, was on stage at the Venice Film Festival. Chaplin was too frail and old to have a conversation, but even that silent meeting left a deep impression on my father. On another occasion, he was delighted that Chaplin's granddaughter visited him in Calcutta at our Beltala flat.

Finally, his ability to concentrate enough to write also faded away. He started to lose his ability to comprehend complex conversations. He could follow everyday topics, but the moment the topics entered more complex and conceptual terrain, I could see in his eyes a sense of being lost. He would try to focus his mind but in vain. He would either continue to stare or force the conversation to move someplace else.

In 2010, *Khandhar* was invited to the prestigious Cannes Classics section. I could see that my father was eager to attend his favourite festival one last time. My mother was too ill to travel, so Nisha and I decided to accompany him. He was very happy to show us all his favourite corners. We celebrated his eighty-seventh birthday with a small group of friends in a restaurant. They reminisced about when, in 1983, his sixtieth birthday had been celebrated with a big rooftop party, with fireworks lighting up the sky above the French Riviera.

During our stay, many press groups wanted to interview him, and we managed to avoid most of them. However, one group convinced him to do a video interview that they wanted to include in a documentary they were planning to make. They used the back patio of our hotel, as it had a quiet seating area. It turned out to be a total disaster, as Bondhu could not understand most of their questions, partly because of his hearing, partly due to their accent, but above all, because he could not process the complicated questions. Therefore, most of his answers were not exactly related to their question. Realizing the difficulty, they wrapped up the session early, and my father knew he had failed, which devastated him. It was a very sad moment for me, and I wished I had never let it happen.

On another occasion, a US distributor of international films asked me to record an interview with him during my visit to Calcutta. The intent was to use an edited version as an introduction to a television screening of *Genesis*. He gave me the questions. In Calcutta, I organized someone to record the interview. We were to do it in our living room one afternoon. When the camera equipment was set, my father came and sat in his favourite chair, but he came with three pages of written answers. He knew he would have difficulty doing it extempore, and preferred to do it in writing; and the written answers were very good. As the camera started to roll, he tried to follow his script, and frequently looked down at his papers. Eventually, he started reading. I printed the text in a bigger font and tried to do an improvised prompting system by holding the pages next to the camera so he could read without lowering his gaze. That did not work either, and he was getting increasingly nervous and embarrassed. After a while, we gave up the whole thing. I lied to him that we had enough to get what we needed. I think he knew I was lying.

The last decade and a half were very rough on me. His mental and physical health were declining. My mother was practically bedridden after a couple of strokes, and when my father broke his hip a second time, we had to hire two nurses to take care of them, day and night. The frequency of our trips had to be increased. Nisha and I would take turns and visit every three or four months. We had to maintain a fleet of people to take care of them—two nurses, a cook and general help, someone to clean the house twice a day, a driver and a part-time person to take care of the bills, medications and all other chores.

We lost the ability to have any private conversation with them, as they were constantly surrounded by people. Whatever privacy they had, we robbed from them when I had no choice but to install a little remote camera between the dining room and their bedroom. This was my lame way of keeping an eye on things while I was away. Even managing their group of helpers was getting difficult. There were conflicts and the inevitability of workplace politics. One day I got a phone call from the person who cooked—she was going to stop working from the next day. That was a terrible crisis because that meant they wouldn't get any food to eat. There was a constant struggle to make things work, and that too over the phone.

In all this, our biggest support was Bondhu's younger friend Dr Adhrishya Kumar. They became close towards the last few decades of his life. A doctor by profession, Adhrishya-da came with a long background of leftist political activism. Every morning, Bondhu's day would start with a phone call with him, and he was always there by my father's side for any need. Every time my father wanted to go to a public event, Adhrishya-da was there. For any medical needs, which was constantly increasing, Adhrishya-da would summon his network of medical professionals. When I was at a loss trying to manage this organization remotely, he was there to help.

While Bondhu's mental health deteriorated, he suffered two setbacks—he fell on two occasions, fracturing one side of his hip and then the other. After his first hip replacement, he still had a strong desire to get better and followed all the instructions of his surgeon friend, Dr Abhijit Sarbadhikary. This effort paid off, and he was almost back to his normal level of movement. However, the second hip replacement broke something deep inside, and he went into a phase of depression and had no desire to do any of the right things. While in hospital, for the first time in my life, I saw him break down and cry inconsolably. He was tired of this existence, and never fully got out of it.

During this period, my mother's health was also declining rapidly. She was mentally sharp till the end, except for some memory issues. But a series of strokes made her progressively less able to move around. She was also depressed and lost her appetite. The low level of nutrition accelerated her physical decline.

On one occasion, during a heavy downpour late one evening, my mother suffered a massive stroke. They were talking to each other after dinner when it happened. This was before they had the nurses; by that time, the other household help were also gone. My father called the neighbourhood doctor. He somehow came, despite the waterlogged streets, and diagnosed it as a cerebral stroke and advised immediate hospitalization. He called a few friends, but no one could help due to the weather. He never thought of calling us that night and just waited, watching my mother in a state of partial paralysis and confusion. Finally, in the morning, someone organized a car to take her to hospital, a full eight hours after, when immediate hospitalization is strictly needed after a stroke.

This single event made my father extremely fearful for my mother's health. I tried to explain to him that his biggest mistake had been to not call me immediately. Even though far away, I would have found a way to mobilize my friends and take care of the situation. I could see that in his helpless state, he wasn't thinking straight. Later, the then chief minister also told him that if he had just called, he would have found a way to use the police trucks or a special ambulance to get her to hospital, despite the late hours and waterlogged streets. There were many resources he could have summoned, but my father could only think of himself, alone, taking care of my mother. He sounded pathetic and lonely.

As my mother's physical health deteriorated, he made care-giving his primary responsibility. He could not do much himself, but that became the new focus of his life. My mother, on the other hand, always believed that my father was incapable of taking care of himself and tried to look after him even when she could hardly get out of bed. They still fought, as all couples do, but there was greater empathy and understanding. As the external world faded out of existence, their world progressively shrank to a tiny cosmos of two people. I visited them every few months, and the day I returned to Chicago, my father would ask me for the date of my next visit. Yet, when I went there, the earlier excitement and joy were gone. It was replaced by relief, because they did not have to worry about each other for the next two weeks. Every time I left Calcutta, I could not avoid the thought that this could be the last time I would see them. Yet, time and again, I would be proven wrong, and they were always there until they were not.

The last time my mother had a stroke, it was massive. She was hospitalized immediately, and I reached Calcutta a day later. She was unconscious when I reached her. She had been moved from one hospital to a nursing home nearer to our home. After a couple of weeks, the doctors agreed that she was unlikely to regain her consciousness and therefore it would be better for her to come back home. The bedroom transformed into a hospital with various machines supplying oxygen, measuring her vital parameters, keeping her air passage clear. During all this time, my father slept in his hospital-style bed next to her, silently watching the flurry of activity.

I had to return to Chicago for a few days as Nisha was also recovering from a serious spinal-cord infection. Though out of a long hospital stay, she also needed my help. After a couple of weeks, I went back to Calcutta. That same afternoon, my mother's life-support system could not keep her alive any more. My father was taking a nap in his bed right next to her. The nurse took him, as usual, to his dining room chair for his afternoon tea. That is when we broke the news to him, news that we had been preparing to deliver for the last three months. For me, it was a relief, as I did not want to see her suffer any more. But we were not sure if my father even understood what was going on.

The doctor came in and wrote the death certificate. Relatives and friends started to pour in. However, mostly to protect Bondhu, we decided to cremate her as soon as possible, and we took her out of the house in less than an hour. My father just stared at every-thing, with no obvious reaction. I came back home as soon as pos-sible, and found my father still sitting in the same dining-room chair, surrounded by a crowd of friends and relatives. At the sight of me, he asked, 'Where is Gita?'

In the following months and years, he was in that twilight zone of knowing and not knowing her absence. He would often wake up and ask about my mother. We later concluded that he may have seen her in his dreams, and that the dream world was slowly merging with his wakeful hours. When I visited, he occasionally asked me about her, as if I could clarify something that he found mysterious and confusing. I would remind him of her death, and he would nod and accept. Every single time he would walk slowly, with his walker, to the dining-room table, there would always be a long pause when his gaze would turn towards a photograph of my mother on the wall, just behind his chair. He would stare at it for a long time with a questioning and hurt look, and then slowly turn and focus his attention on the difficult task of sitting down.

Even though they rarely spoke to each other towards the end, Bondhu entered a particularly lonely phase after her death. The house was full of caregivers, but he felt alone. Even during my visits, which became much more frequent, he hardly spoke. One day he told me that 'all these people', pointing at the caregivers, 'they are all very nice and take very good care of me, but they are not sophisticated enough.' Even though he could not say much any more, he missed the intellectual discourse that had become absent from our home.

The home that was once filled with visitors at all times of the day had started becoming empty after they moved to the Padma-pukur Road flat. Since he was no longer active as a filmmaker, his colleagues had to work with other production houses and stopped coming regularly. His friends were also getting older and could not make the trip. His younger friends were all busy with their lives and stopped coming. In the end, sometimes a week would go by without any visitors. Those who still came often found him taking a nap or unresponsive and eventually stopped coming.

Only rarely, when some of his favourites would visit, he would perk up and engage with them. His mind started working again, and he would ask the right questions and react exactly how they remembered. These friends would often remark that he hadn't changed. However, the extraordinary energy it demanded left him exhausted after a little while. At this point, he would make it clear that he would prefer them to leave. However brief, these sparks were wonderful to watch.

The person who did everything in his capacity to make each day of his life unique, distinct and exciting entered a phase where each day was the same as the day before. The distinctions between days slowly faded away, the colours turned into shades of grey, and finally, the same tone of dull greyness. This is the biggest tragedy of age, when we can no longer keep our days distinct and surprising.

Back in Chicago, two days before the New Year, I had just finished emailing my annual electronic cards, when the phone rang. Adhrishya-da informed me that he had just received a call from the nurse that my father had a fever and was not responding. He was on his way to our place and wanted to let me know. I immediately told Nisha that we needed to prepare to go home. I purchased our tickets for the next day, just as I received the call that he was no more.

Emails and text messages started pouring in, and social media was ablaze. I went to bed with constant reminders from my phone that the big event I always dreaded was upon us. There was no sleep for us that night, and the next morning was busy responding to the news media. The flight was somewhat comforting as it shielded us from the communication channels.

When we reached home early in the morning, his bed was empty as he had been moved to a funeral home. We decided to cremate him as soon as possible. My father always used to warn us against the idea of any fanfare around his dead body. I also disliked such a display and decided to walk from our home to the crematorium. No public announcement was made, but in the age of social media, the news spread like wildfire. By the time we reached the area, a huge crowd had accumulated. As we started walking towards the crematorium along Rashbehari Avenue, we realized that the traffic police had anticipated it and cordoned off the roads. It was a long and silent procession. I later heard that occasionally people at the flanks of the procession would spontaneously start singing some of his favourite organizing songs from his younger days.

After a few days, we locked up our home and came back to Chicago. For thirty-five years and over a hundred similar trips, the first thing we did after entering our Chicago home was to pick up the phone and let them know that we arrived safely. That was once again my first instinct, but I immediately realized that, for the first time, no one was waiting for that call. For the first time since we'd left Calcutta all those years ago, we now had only one home.

HIS LEGACY

Now that he is gone and people talk about him in the past tense, and about his legacy, I often wonder how much he cared about all that. He certainly enjoyed his celebrity status. Strangely, he believed in his own greatness even before others were convinced of the same. He enjoyed it when he was recognized in a crowd or was treated specially, and he expected people to pay attention. I think he was happy when his work was appreciated by others, even though he rarely showed it. But he never showed any interest in preserving his legacy.

There was little he could do to preserve his films, and all his life, he witnessed copies of his films getting damaged or lost. In the pre-video and pre-digital era, the only way to preserve a film was by keeping a copy of a celluloid print. This was an impossible task, not only because he was not the rights owner of most of his films but also because prints were expensive to make. Even if he could get a copy, they were big and bulky and could not be stored at home. Since my teenage years, I remember the task of hauling these huge, battered tin trunks up and down our stairs as prints arrived from film festivals. We could store them temporarily, one copy at a time, but storing many would have required a special storage area with air-conditioning and humidity control. Of course, that was impossible, and all he could do was to watch them getting lost.

Towards the end of 2022, I received an email from the Film Heritage Foundation, saying that they tried to recover the original negatives of *Khandhar* from Prasad Film Laboratories in Chennai, the professional keepers of the film, and had received the following response:

> With ref to the below, we wish to inform you that the final picture and sound negatives (Reel Nos. 1 to 11) of the film KHANDHAR - Hindi are totally decomposed and not usable for any purpose due to its ageing.

If a professional laboratory could not save a copy, there was little chance they would have survived the conditions of a regular home.

However, taking care of his papers was within his means, and yet I did not see him ever trying to save them. He never cared to save copies of his screenplays or his writing. They were always piled up in haphazard ways that included the important with the useless. When my mother screamed at him, he would tie a rope around a bundle and shove it somewhere, under the bed or on top of a shelf, before he was forced to throw them away. He never kept a copy of any of the articles he wrote before he handed the original manuscript over to the publisher. That is, it never occurred to him that someday someone may want to compile them. The same thing happened with his letters. Not only did he never try to keep copies of what he wrote, he also did not try to save the ones he received, even those that were obviously valuable. This reminds me of my friend Dipu's comment about Tagore's collected letters, which filled entire volumes. Dipu theorized that Tagore must have put a sheet of carbon paper when writing each letter, or else how could the editors collect all his outgoing mail?

While moving from our Beltala home to Padmapukur, there was the massive task of deciding what to take and what to discard.

Bondhu was tasked with sorting his hundreds of bundles. This proved to be an impossible task, and instead of going over dozens of years of disorganized papers, he found it easier to throw them out. So he requested the Calcutta Municipal Corporation to send a garbage truck, to carry away them all away. By the time I arrived, all the packages were gone. At some point, the Corporation men came to my mother and reported that one of the discarded sacks sounded like it had metal inside. She discovered that it was full of dozens of minor awards and trophies. When the move was finished, every piece of paper of any value was already in a garbage dump somewhere or being converted into paper bags. Not a single screenplay, letter, article or manuscript survived this purge.

In his lifetime, my father became important enough to know that these things may acquire some value over time. I am sure he could imagine that people may one day want to publish his correspondences, screenplays and articles. Yet, there was no attempt to preserve them. It is hard to attribute it all to his disorganized nature. If that were the case, we would have seen poorly organized bundles of important papers. Instead, what we see is a total lack of any attempt to preserve anything. Yet, it was not a conscious or philosophical decision not to save. I could never understand his attitude.

We had thousands of books on our bookshelves, including many autographed and gifted by prominent authors. People always borrowed books from him, and they seldom returned them; the signed books especially never found a way back home. The same thing happened with his photographs. Every time he went to some film festival or other, he returned with a bundle of photographs gifted to him. We never had a second copy of these photographs. Bondhu would let magazine and book publishers borrow these photographs, but they rarely came back. Any unusual photo I see in one such book or magazine, I seldom find the same original in the pile of photographs that he kept on a bookshelf. On several occasions, Nisha tried to organize these photographs in separate airtight bags with meaningful labels. Bondhu was very appreciative of the labour she put in and the convenience of the result, but when we returned a few months later, the organization was mostly lost.

After his death, a few organizations showed interest in archiving his papers. Unfortunately, there was very little to give. The few things of some value were what I had with me in Chicago— letters between me and my parents, some articles and clippings, and some of his major awards that were stored in a bank vault. When the University of Chicago approached me to archive them in their special collection, I immediately agreed. I faced some criticism about my decision, since it would have been more appropriate to keep them in India. I cannot disagree with such sentiments, but I could not find an organization there that had the infrastructure for long-term archiving. Some of his materials went to the Film Heritage Foundation in Mumbai. This is an exceptionally professional organization that maintains an archive of film artefacts, founded and run by Shivendra Singh Dungarpur—a passionate and competent individual with great international connections. My only concern is what will happen to this organization when he is no longer there to run it. Indian organizations often cannot make the leap from an individual enterprise to an institution. I sincerely hope that I am wrong. The same can be said about a wonderful archive that Arindam Saha Sardar created in his own space in Uttarpara. However, I feel most confident that whatever I left with the University of Chicago Library will remain intact even after two hundred years, in case anyone has an interest in finding them.

Will anyone be interested in him or his work fifty years from now, a hundred years, two hundred? This is a tough question. The value of an artist depends largely on the prevailing social mindscape of the future, and that is very hard to predict.

Looking back, I often wonder: What were his true contributions? What did he do that truly distinguished him from others? I can think of a few things. The most distinguishing characteristic was his experimentation with the form. He was probably the first Indian filmmaker who challenged the usual storytelling tradition of Indian cinema with his *Bhuvan Shome*. Around that time, there were a few other filmmakers who also tried to break away from tradition, like Mani Kaul and Kumar Sahani. Those movements gradually fizzled out, but he consistently continued to experiment. Structurally, films like *Interview, Calcutta 71, Chorus, Chalchitra, Genesis, Mahaprithibi* and *Antareen* are distinct from most other Indian films.

Whether his experiments worked or not is something the audience has to say, but it cannot be questioned that his film language had a distinct tone, and that it kept changing. Generally, the Indian audience was never comfortable with anything outside of a simply told, wholesome story. That is very disappointing to me. After a performance in India, a popular, international music group once said about the Indian audience, 'Others know what they like, but Indians like what they know,' which is an apt description. Recently, I was present during the screening of *Interview* at a US university. It was wonderful to see how the audience reacted, not only to the political content of the film but also to its language. Therefore, there is a chance that even a hundred years from now, film scholars may take an interest in the formal experimentations he tried to introduce into the Indian film scene.

Most creative artists search for a language, a style. Once they discover a voice that is distinctive and appreciated, they tend to stick to it. This is certainly a sound strategy. Very few artists have the courage to deviate from their well-tested formula. One thing that distinguishes my father as a filmmaker is his courage to seek new ways to express his ideas. Every time he found a new language, he would make a few films in that style, and then discard it and search for a new one. This happened many times in his career, and that, I believe, is truly remarkable. Perhaps he could have perfected his craft if he had stayed with a single, successful style. But perfection was never something that attracted him, and he was always eager to try something new. He did not feel challenged enough if he settled into a comfort zone. He preferred running to walking. Constantly about to fall, he would recover at the last moment only to initiate another fall.

The other aspect of his films that characterized him was his politics. The films he made in the seventies were explicitly political. Sometimes the intent was propaganda, sometimes criticism, sometimes analysis. I believe that the longevity of political art depends largely on the continued validity of the politics with which the art is concerned. If the audience feels it is still a valid political issue, or is at least curious about those politics, then the art remains interesting. But if society loses all interest in that brand of politics, or they are convinced that it is no longer relevant, then the art is also forgotten. For example, in the current political environment in many parts of the world, there is a renewed interest in fascism, and art that dealt with this issue seventy years ago is being rediscovered. Marxist politics is slowly ebbing away from public consciousness, but who can tell if people will find it interesting again in the future? Some of my father's films from this period may also act as a record of history, and people may revisit them to understand that period.

Many of the films he made in the eighties were explorations and autopsies of contemporary lower-middle-class society. These films may retain some relevance since this class will be present in our societies for a long time. The specific details may change, but there is probably some central truth that these films capture that will remain meaningful. For example, *Ek Din Pratidin*. When the film was shown in Western countries, where a single woman staying out for the night is not such a remarkable incident, one would think that the story, and its main concern, would fail to make any sense. However, that was not the case, and when my father asked some of his Western friends this question, they all said they could understand the crisis perfectly well. I think it shows that films like *Ek Din Pratidin* or *Kharij* touch upon deeper realities that go beyond the physical and temporal milieu and, therefore, may remain relevant in the future.

Films like *Khandhar* or *Antareen* are more introspective at a personal level and may have the best chance of reaching across time. These films talk about some fundamental human emotions, like loneliness, isolation, hope and betrayal, that cut across time and geography. It is no surprise that *Khandhar* was picked by Cannes in their Cannes Classics series since its appeal is universal, and it may withstand the test of time. The narrative structure of films like *Antareen* or *Chalchitra* are far less conventional and generally appeals to a smaller audience; they are almost absent from the Indian scene. Personally, I find *Chalchitra* to be one of his most modern films, but it was rarely watched in India.

In 2023, my father would have been a hundred. He came close to witnessing it himself, but in a way I am glad he didn't. He was in no shape to face all the attention he might have got. We tried to keep him away from the media during the last few years of his life. We wanted him to be remembered as a person who was sharp and quick in his thinking and not as someone who lost his battle with time. Unfortunately, we could not always protect him. Only a few understood that even celebrities have the right to a time when the world becomes small and private. All my life, we shared him with the rest of the world, but at the very end, he was just Bondhu to Nisha and me, Mrinal-da to his closest friends and Baba to his caregivers.

Memories that are captured externally, like photographs, get condensed into tangible bits, and they slowly float away from our personal memories. After a long time, all we can remember are the photographs, not the reality. For people with public lives, their memories slowly move from the privacy of a few people into public memories. My father's existence as a filmmaker was always public, as we can hear and read through magazine articles, books and other public anecdotes. Beyond that are the more intimate stories, but they too gradually get diffused into the public space. Everything I wrote here was private and intimate until now, but no more. I have truly personal memories with Nisha, but I cannot say the same about my father; I have no desire for exclusive possession and, therefore, no regrets.

The only thing that remains strictly intimate are the intangible memories. I still remember the slightly acrid and musty smell of my father's body. I remember the smell of my mother as a mixture of turmeric, spices and a jasmine perfume that she loved. I remember the touch of their skin and their gestures and subtle expressions. Above all, I will always remain the sole viewer of the living mental image of my father. This simulation can do and say things he may have never done or said, but it feels just like him. This is the man I see in my dreams. With time, my parents will be reduced to just these few unshareable things that are directly connected to my senses and my mind. For the rest, I will remember them as a collection of stories, photographs and videos, just as everyone else.